To
Emily and Lucy

CONTENTS

PREFACE

This book is written to help nurses develop the ability to appreciate the techniques used in undertaking behavioural research and to enable them to acquire further knowledge about human behaviour which can be applied in their work. The development of 'research-mindedness' is now recognized to be fundamental to the professional role of the nurse. To be research-minded means being able to understand the procedures and implement the findings of research in a careful and critical manner. Knowledge about human behaviour is increasingly stressed as being important to nursing but it has often been overshadowed in nurse education by the traditional emphasis on the medical and physical aspects of caring for people.

The most important feature of this book is the inclusion of a series of practicals which we have designed to help nurses learn for themselves how psychologists investigate human behaviour. These practicals will involve the reader using a wide range of research techniques which have been related to the context of nursing. Carrying out these practicals will enable the reader to examine critically the strengths and weaknesses of different investigative techniques. Sometimes in the course of their work nurses may have to be involved in research with patients or apply some of the findings from research already conducted. This is impossible to do if they do not have an understanding of the processes involved in research.

We will not of course be asking nurses to try out these practicals on patients. They are designed to be carried out with groups drawn from friends and colleagues or sometimes from the general public. Each practical in this book has been carried out successfully with a group of nurses. We did this with undergraduate nurses, student nurses and a group of qualified nurses studying for the Diploma in Nursing. We have included a number of practicals to be carried out as class activities which a tutor could organize and some which individuals can do alone, or in small groups. It is not vital to involve a tutor, however, and groups of nurses can organize themselves to try out the practicals. To help the reader do this we indicate when one person needs to be the 'experimenter' with access to information which others should not have. No special apparatus is required except pencil and paper and occasionally a watch with a second hand. Sometimes it will be helpful to have a room in which a space can be cleared to allow for discussion groups. The practicals do not necessarily have to be carried out in the precise order given in the book but to some extent the earlier chapters provide the foundation for the later ones.

Having carried out a particular practical we think it is helpful for individuals to write it up. This is not vital but enhances the value of the practical as a whole. We provide a guide to writing up practicals in Chapter 8. There are no statistical tests of significance in the book as we have concentrated on particular research techniques. However, in Appendix VIII we list some statistical procedures which could be applied to some of the practicals in case individuals want to take this step. The purpose of our book is not to ignore the need to test the significance of research findings, but to help all nurses to begin to appreciate the research process in relation to human behaviour and nursing. The main point is that this is a book which is intended for all nurses and not just those who want to become researchers. We hope nurses will enjoy using it and discover more about human behaviour and their work.

We would like to express our gratitude to all the colleagues and friends who have encouraged us in writing this book, and especially to the following people who have been involved in its preparation: Jackie Carter, Jennifer Fry, Julia Hawkins, Yvonne Wattley, Eileen Webb, Vik Müller, Denise Ryan, Joe Waddle (senior), Alex Waddle, Graham Wattley and all our students including Lynne Broome, Catherine Emmott, Anne Hemmingway and Geraint Morgan. We are also very grateful to Christine Chapman for writing the Foreword. Finally we would like to acknowledge the generous support and enthusiasm of Cathy Peck, Senior Editor, Harper and Row Publishers.

FOREWORD

It has become something of a truism to state 'nursing must become a research-based profession' and the response of many is 'but how?'. While it might be desirable, it is unlikely that all nurses will be able to be involved actively in research but all can, and should, be able to read research and appreciate the methods used. This book is produced to enable 'research-mindedness' to develop in nurses at all levels and, at the same time, a knowledge and understanding of human behaviour by using psychological concepts.

The method used is unusual in that the reader is expected to complete various practical exercises and experiments, which will assist his or her ability to construct and use the tools of behavioural science research, at the same time as assisting in the understanding of the psychological concepts and their application to nursing.

Both authors are well qualified to adopt this approach. Lesley Wattley is a qualified nurse and a developmental psychologist, teaching nursing undergraduates both nursing and psychology. Dave Müller is a psychologist teaching (among others) nurses undertaking postbasic nursing education, such as the Diploma in Nursing. All the practical exercises have been tested by them on their students and therefore the reader is assured of their practicality and validity.

It gives me great pleasure to be associated with this exciting development in textbooks, which nurses and their teachers will find fills a long-felt gap.

I wish the venture of writing, reading, doing and learning, well.

C. M. Chapman, BSc, MPhil, SRN, SCM, RNT, FRCN
Director of Nursing Studies

CHAPTER 1

PSYCHOLOGY AND NURSING

On being introduced to the study of psychology it is quite common for nurses to think that what they are being taught is simply a matter of common sense. In the course of their everyday work nurses have to make important decisions which affect the welfare of others, and in doing this they use knowledge about human beings, some of which might be called psychological. If they have to calm a distressed relative or try and persuade patients to help themselves toward recovery by, for example, moving around while in bed, their experience of human behaviour may make it easier for them to help more effectively. Nurses familiar with these kinds of situations may well feel that they are using psychology anyway, even though they have never studied it. After all it would seem very strange if in working with other people one did not use one's own understanding of human behaviour. It would be even more strange if the work of psychologists continually rejected common sense viewpoints of human behaviour. If it did, those of us who work in the caring professions would surely be ineffective in our work. However, psychology is not the same thing as common sense.

When discussing common sense knowledge of behaviour we are often referring implicitly to so-called 'normal' behaviour. How do people know what is 'normal behaviour'? Experience and common sense provide a rough guide, or rule of thumb; just as touching someone's forehead may give a rough idea about whether they are feverish. Nurses usually prefer a more accurate assessment of a person's temperature to decide on an appropriate treatment and, unless they know what the normal range of body temperature is, they cannot describe someone as pyrexial.

In terms of behaviour the same thing applies. Nurses need to understand the normal psychological functions of everyday human behaviour 'which form a vital component of the individual's health (Crow 1976, p.54) to recognize when someone's psychological reaction to a situation is abnormal. Unless nurses appreciate the normal range of behaviour they cannot take steps to prevent abnormal reactions from occurring, or summon skilled psychological help when necessary.

Nursing and psychology have overlapping interests. There is much to be gained from psychologists investigating nursing and from nurses investigating psychology. Working in the 'real world' of nursing enables psychologists to develop further their insights into human behaviour and to test their knowledge to see whether their findings really are practical. Nurses, on the other hand, by investigating psychology are able to refine and develop their experience and common sense knowledge of behaviour and understand better how to work effectively with their patients and others. Because psychology and nursing are both concerned with human beings they share the difficulties of finding acceptable ways of studying them.

What is nursing?

It has proved difficult to provide an exact and satisfactory description of nursing. Henderson (1960) suggests that

'Nursing is primarily assisting the individual (sick or well) in the performance of those activities contributing to health, or its recovery (or to peaceful death) that he would perform unaided if he had the necessary strength, will or knowledge. It is likewise the unique contribution of nursing to help the individual to be independent of such assistance as soon as possible.' (p.3)

More recently, Crow (1976) has stressed the relation between the physical and social sciences in the practice of nursing. The aim of nursing is described as 'maintaining optimal physiological and psychological functioning' in patients (p.52). This enterprise is clearly empirical, meaning that it is based on observation and evaluation. A certain way of dealing with a situation is tried and its effectiveness evaluated. To return to the analogy with taking a temperature to measure the degree of pyrexia, a nurse may decide to provide a pyrexial patient with an electric fan, or reduce the number of blankets. There would be little point doing this unless the nurse returned to see if the measures had been effective by taking the patient's temperature again. On the basis of the new information the nurse would decide if further measures should be used or the existing ones modified.

The need for evaluation in nursing is a fundamental tenet of the nursing process on which great emphasis has been placed in recent years (Roper et al. 1981; McFarlane & Castledine 1982). The nursing process offers nurses a breakdown of stages necessary for ensuring that care is appropriate and effective. It involves assessing the needs of patients initially and at any time in their care, since their needs may change continually. On the basis of the assessment, a plan of care to meet the patient's needs can be drawn up, and modified according to the findings of further assessments. The plan describes any interventions which may be necessary to ensure optimal physiological and psychological functioning of the individual (Crow 1976), including any treatments required as part of the medical regimen. An important aspect of the whole process is then the evaluation of the effectiveness of the interventions. Evaluation is not reserved for discussion after the patient is discharged; it is an ongoing important aspect of the patient's continuing care and it always involves 'comparison against an objective' (Roper et al. 1981, p.5). In other words, what was wanted in the first place (discovered through assessment) is compared with the actual outcome. A 'measure' of effectiveness is thus obtained.

It is clear, however, that if nursing is concerned with the needs of individuals, assessment will involve both physical and psychological aspects. Nurses collect all kinds of data about people. Physical measurements of temperature, pulse, respirations and blood pressure are, for example, recorded and used to build up a picture of the physical condition of the patient and to determine subsequent actions. Many nurses might recognize psychological states such as anxiety from accompanying physical signs, including sweating and trembling, and increased needs to micturate or defecate. However, at a more speculative level nurses also learn to recognize and respond to the whole range of human emotions such as humour, grief and loneliness.

Interestingly, as described by Johnston (1976), while nurses do seem to know the sorts of things which worry patients in general, they do not demonstrate an ability to know which particular patients worry about which particular things (p.37). In other words, the nurses' psychological understanding is general. Although it is customary to describe the concern of nursing as 'the individual' and his or her own particular needs, this evidence suggests that nurses are not skilled in assessing the actual psychological needs of a particular individual. Another important finding is that nurses tend to overestimate the psychological suffering of patients, which they infer from the patients behaviour (p.35). This is important because it highlights the lack of a systematic approach to the measurement of behaviour.

Psychologists try to measure many of the behaviours of human beings, including those met by nurses in their work, and thus contribute to the knowledge available for the nursing profession. However, psychology can seem confusing and ambiguous if its methods of investigation are not understood. The next section clarifies the scope of psychology further.

What is psychology?

Psychology is primarily concerned with the systematic and objective study of human behaviour. Its focus of interest is on the individual and on trying to understand how and why individuals behave the way they do. This concern with individual behaviour makes the subject matter of psychology similar to that of nursing (see, e.g. Henderson 1960). It follows that the knowledge acquired by psychologists is often of immediate relevance to nurses especially when patterns of behaviour common to many individuals are identified. For example, however willing doctors are to inform patients about their condition and to give advice, research has shown that patients still forget a great deal of the information given to them (Ley 1979, 1981). Ley has worked extensively on this problem; he has been able to suggest solutions and ways in which in practice patients can be helped to remember more information (see Chapter 6).

The study of psychology is characterized by its emphasis on scientific methodology. A science has three broad distinguishing criteria. First, it is *empirical* being based on observable and testable data, rather than on opinions or beliefs which are subjective. Hence there is an emphasis on objectivity. Secondly, psychologists *measure* behaviour to collect reliable data as evidence. If it is reliable, the same measures would be recorded by anybody carrying out the same investigation. Psychologists attempt to find ways of measuring even the most elusive concepts such as intelligence, personality and interpersonal communication. Finally, psychologists work *systematically* and attempt to build theories and models explaining behaviour. In doing this they generate ideas which can be tested empirically in order that they can either be invalidated or shown to be accurate.

However, this does not mean that psychologists necessarily share a common view of what people are like. Chapman & Jones (1980) have put together a wide range of viewpoints from many leading British psychologists of models of human behaviour. Beloff (1973) has argued convincingly that there is no single science called psychology, but rather a number of psychological sciences all with their own focus of study. Orr (1979) has made a similar point in relation to the study of nursing. In a challenging paper she argues that nurses need to be aware of rival and differing philosophies about the nature of 'man', the goal of nursing, the identification of nursing activities and the role of the nurse.

Such differing perspectives can be considered a strength rather than a weakness, since psychology can offer different ways of investigating behaviour objectively. This is of particular importance in applying psychology to health-care settings (Müller 1980, 1981). This apparent ambiguity may seem difficult for nurses to accept. On the other hand, there has been a tradition in nursing of looking at things in 'black and white' terms, yet people cannot be easily categorized, physically, socially or psychologically. As Crow (1980) has noted, 'social sciences require tolerance of ambiguity for their clearest understanding' (p.6). The key point is that these differing viewpoints and methods of inquiry are characterized by a critical approach and an emphasis on evaluation (Wattley & Müller 1983a). This emphasis is of particular interest in considering the relation between psychology and nursing as has been illustrated by a series of papers (Janforum 1983; Wattley & Müller 1983b).

Need for research

From our discussion of nursing and psychology it can be seen that both nurses and psychologists collect information and use it to make informed decisions. In this way both disciplines are clearly empirical. It follows that scientific methodology should be an integral part of both psychology and nursing. This has long been recognized in psychology, but it is only during the last few decades that the nursing profession has given it much emphasis. It is rather ironic that Florence Nightingale's commitment to scientific techniques seems to have been forgotten. As Simpson (1971) has noted, this research approach to nursing problems has never been transmitted as part of the Nightingale tradition.

To some extent the recent emphasis on research in nursing reflects the desire nursing has to demonstrate its professional status (Briggs 1972; Hockey 1980; RCN 1982). As Hockey has argued, 'a research commitment is one of the most important hallmarks of a profession', and she states that 'the science of nursing comes from research' (1980 p.10).

However, the most recent report on 'research-mindedness' from the professional body (RCN 1982) notes 'that although lip-service is paid to the importance of nurses becoming research-minded, in practice the knowledge and understanding within the profession is increasing only slowly' (p.1).

In practice then, what is meant by the term 'research-mindedness'? The Royal College of Nursing (RCN 1982) stresses the development of a critical and questioning approach and similar qualities have been discussed by Hockey (1980), Lelean (1980a, b) and Wattley (1982). Certainly the methods of psychology are characterized by this sort of approach (see Müller 1981) and as such provide a useful resource for nursing.

The Briggs report (1972) makes it clear that, in any profession, full-time research is the responsibility of a minority, but everyone else needs to have 'a sense of the need for research'. Lelean (1980a, b) has interpreted this as meaning that all nurses should be able to read and assess research findings and be prepared to examine their own practice in view of these findings. Clark & Hockey (1979) argue that 'to make use of research does not necessarily mean to implement findings' (p.4) but that it does imply the ability to read research reports critically.

Van Bree (1981) has argued that students are more likely to develop positive attitudes toward research when they learn by actually doing a small project of their own. In this book we intend to introduce the reader to some aspects of psychology relevant to nursing by demonstrating the techniques used by psychologists in conducting research. The reader will be encouraged to carry out practicals to develop an understanding of the process of research and the characteristics of research-mindedness. Because of the nature of the book the nurse will also gain psychological knowledge relevant to the context of nursing.

Practical 1.1 Identifying potential safety hazards in a hospital environment

Introduction

As we have already seen both nurses and psychologists place great emphasis on collecting information or data. One obvious way of doing this is of course by observation. In their everyday work nurses rely a great deal on their ability to observe. One area in which they should become skilled concerns the safety of patients, staff and others. An awareness of potential dangers involves psychological processes such as learning and perception. Information is received and interpreted and on the basis of this decisions are made.

For example, on a surgical ward, nurses will be particularly alert to the possibility of haemorrhage occurring postoperatively in say patients having abdominal surgery. They learn that through certain observations haemorrhaging can be detected. Consequently, nurses will take recordings of pulse rate and blood pressure. At the same time they will note the colour of the patient's skin, what it feels like to touch and the appearance of the wound site. They may suspect haemorrhaging on the basis of one or more observations: a sudden change in pulse rate and blood pressure; a trend in which the pulse is rising and the blood pressure is falling; signs of bleeding at the wound site; drainage bottles filling rapidly; signs of swelling or bruising of the tissues around the wound site; increasing pain reported by the patient; by sweating or the pallor of the patient's skin. If alert, nurses can initiate action to avoid a disaster. The combination of past learning and experience (knowledge) with perception (the interpretation of observations) serves, in this context, to protect the surgical patient. The practical that follows has been designed to investigate some of the processes involved in observation.

Method

This practical can be carried out with the class as subjects, but it is also interesting to try it out on other groups of subjects who are not nurses. For our study we used a group of 22 experienced nurses who were studying for the Diploma in Nursing, 14 first-year degree-course nurses in their first week of training and a group of 10 speech-therapy degree students. We expected to find differences between the groups in their ability to identify potential hazards in a nursing environment.

There is in Appendix I a line drawing of a hospital ward. You should not look at this or at Table 1.1 on page 9, until you have read and carried out the following instructions:

> In the picture that we are going to show you there are a number of hazards preventing the maintenance of a safe environment. You are going to be given 3 minutes to write down as many of these hazards as you can. Now turn to Appendix I on p.138.

Results

One mark was awarded for each hazard correctly identified. The full list appears in Table 1.1. In our study we made allowance for ambiguities in the drawing; for example, the spill on the floor was scored as correct if it was identified as a handkerchief or a rag. No extra marks were awarded for the identification of other potential hazards. Table 1.1 shows how many students within each group correctly identified each hazard. To compare the three groups mean scores for each were calculated. The mean is calculated by dividing the total score for each group by the number of students in each group; for example, the diploma in nursing students scored a total of 340 points and as there were 22 of them, the mean was $340/22 = 15.5$. These data are presented in Table 1.2. The range of scores is also given which shows the smallest number of correct identifications made by anybody in that group and the largest. In our study we found that there were considerable differences between the mean scores for each group and in the range of scores.

Discussion

Our results indicate that the more experienced nurses were able to identify more hazards. Their mean score was higher than for either of the other groups. The least successful group was, as we expected, the speech-therapy students, although their age and A-level qualifications were similar to the first-year group of nursing students. These results give some indication of the role of experience in helping identify potential hazards on the ward. However, they are also encouraging to less experienced nurses who seem to be well 'tuned' in to the kinds of problem they might have to deal with. Perhaps if longer than 3 minutes were allowed, our first-year nursing students might have identified more of the hazards. Experience might just help us work faster. You could test this idea yourself by repeating the experiment with new subjects and allowing more time.

Looking at Table 1.1 more closely, one can observe some interesting points. All groups were good at noticing the open and unattended drug trolley, but only the experienced nurses fully appreciated the significance of a syringe with an unguarded needle. Only two-thirds of the nursing students recognized this and half of the speech-therapy students. A similar pattern of results occurred with the patient drinking despite a 'nil orally' sign on his bed. Experienced nurses presumably have learnt to

Table 1.1 Numbers of students within each group correctly identifying hazards

Hazard	DN (n = 22)	N (n = 14)	ST (n = 10)
1. Unattended open drug trolley	22	13	8
2. Unguarded syringe	22	10	5
3. Keys lying on trolley	13	7	6
4. Nurse carrying uncovered used bedpan	13	7	5
5. Patient drinking although 'nil orally' sign up	19	7	6
6. Patient on bed with legs crossed below knee	13	1	0
7. Dead flowers in vase	9	8	6
8. Overflowing rubbish bin	21	14	6
9. Overflowing dirty linen skip	21	14	7
10. Crumpled used sheet on clean trolley	21	7	6
11. Intravenous infusion bag without stand	20	12	5
12. Pills on locker	15	5	5
13. Nurse with wrist-watch and ring	14	13	5
14. Spill on floor	20	14	8
15. Fire door wedged open	22	13	8
16. Flex trailing to fan	22	14	7
17. Cigarette burning	22	14	10
18. False teeth on locker	13	4	2
19. Shoes on bed	1	3	3
20. Slippers in way on floor	17	11	6

DN, Diploma in nursing students; N, first-year degree nurses; ST, speech-therapy students.

Table 1.2 Means and range of scores for each group

	DN (n = 22)	N (n = 14)	ST (n = 10)
Total scores	340	191	114
Range	11–19	11–16	9–15
Means	15.5	13.6	11.4

DN, Diploma in nursing students; N, first-year degree nurses; ST, speech-therapy students.

check whether the sign is being violated as a matter of course. Another hazard requires more technical knowledge: the man with his lower legs crossed was identified as sitting in a potentially hazardous way by experienced nurses, but not by the other groups. This relates to knowledge about the risk of blood vessel compression and pooling in deep veins which may lead to deep vein thrombosis. A spill on the floor, on the other hand, would be a hazard in any environment and was recognized by the whole sample. Another point of particular interest concerns the nurse in the picture wearing a wrist-watch and ring. The nursing students did very well on this point, perhaps surprisingly, but the previous day they had received information on the dangers to patients of wearing these while on duty. This then demonstrates the importance of expectation or being 'set' to observe something specific. Only two-thirds of the experienced nurses noticed this hazard; only one nursing student failed to.

The results confirm what we would expect but yet illustrate a number of important points about observation. Experience clearly plays an important role, although at times being prepared to look for something specific is of greater significance. Speed of reaction may be another important factor related to experience. It would also have been interesting to see how well these particular groups of subjects remembered the hazards and how accurate they might have been in passing on this information to others. As in any interesting practical, more questions are often raised than actually answered.

Conclusion

Although a useful research tool, observation is unlikely to be entirely objective. We have already shown some of the factors affecting it, including the experience of the observer and the time available. The situation is made more complex if one tries to observe people rather than line drawings. What effect does being observed by someone have on you? People are likely to feel uncomfortable being watched and change their behaviour as a result. A typical example of this in nursing, is assessing a student on a drug round. Every nurse will recall the elaborate preparations made for the assessment so that the clinical teacher will be left in no doubt that the candidate is a safe practitioner. A curious thing sometimes seems to happen later to some nurses, when unconscious of being observed, they perform in a different way.

Whenever nurses are observing another person, at least in the context of their work, they are part of the situation in which they are observing. Hence nurses may be unable to separate the specific effects they have on patients or other staff, from those imposed by the situation itself. In this way nurses are always part of the situation that they are observing and hence are themselves involved.

In undertaking observation studies, researchers normally collect data in one of two ways. The more objective is to develop categories to enable behaviour to be recorded systematically. For example, the observer might wish to record the number and type of request a particular set of patients make, and devise an observation schedule to do this. This kind of approach was adopted by Bales (1970) to investigate small-group behaviour and we will look at this kind of technique in Chapter 5. The other approach is for the observer to deliberately become part of the events being studied, as in a nurse deciding to become a patient in a hospital without those immediately involved being aware of it. This is referred to as participant observation and although it raises ethical and practical problems it often enables deeper insight into the topic of study. Allen (1981) describes a participant observation study carried out in a psychiatric unit. Hall (1978) has discussed in detail the specific relevance of observation techniques to nursing. He describes the strengths and weaknesses of case and ward studies and the recording of specific incidents. He argues that in general such techniques can deepen our understanding. Observation then can be used to investigate a vast number of important aspects of nursing care as long as the difficulties involved in this approach are taken into account. The reader is referred to a more advanced text for a further discussion of these issues (Mook 1982).

One kind of preparation for observation is proposed by Sommer & Sommer (1980) in their handbook on research. They suggest that it might be important for observers to get to know themselves first, in order that they get to know their own biases. The next chapter concentrates on finding out about oneself.

Summary

In this chapter we have considered the relation between nursing and psychology. It was suggested that they involve empirical techniques and that research is of major importance to both the nurse and the psychologist. One technique used in research, that of observation, was the subject of our first practical. This demonstrated among other things the particular significance of experience. Different types of techniques for observing human behaviour were then discussed and the problem of subjectivity introduced. Finally, the importance of observers getting to know themselves was mentioned. This is the focus of the next chapter.

References

Allen, H (1981) 'Voices of Concern' – a study of verbal communication about patients in a psychiatric day unit. *Journal of Advanced Nursing* **6**, 355–362

Bales, R F (1970) *Personality and Interpersonal Behavior* New York: Holt, Rinehart and Winston

Beloff, J (1973) *Psychological Sciences: A Review of Modern Psychology* St Albans: Crosby, Lockwood, Staples

Briggs, A (1972) *Report of the Committee on Nursing* London: Her Majesty's Stationery Office

Chapman, A J & Jones, D M (1980) *Models of Man* Leicester: The British Psychological Society

Clark, J & Hockey, L (1979) *Research for Nursing. A Guide for the Enquiring Nurse* Aylesbury: HM & M

Crow, J (1980) *Effects of Preparation on Problem Solving* London: Royal College of Nursing

Crow, R A (1976) A fresh look at psychology in nursing. *Journal of Advanced Nursing* **1** 51–62

Hall, D J (1978) 'What nurse don't see, she don't worry about' or the use of observation in hospital research. *Nursing Times Occasional Papers* **74**, 137–140

Henderson, V (1960) *Basic Principles of Nursing Care* London: International Council of Nurses

Hockey, L (1980) Challenges for nursing. *Nursing Times* **76**, 908–911

Janforum (1983) *Journal of Advanced Nursing* **8**, 335–342

Johnston, M (1976) Communication of patients' feelings in hospital. In A F Bennett (ed.) *Communication between Doctors and Patients* Nuffield Provincial Hospitals Trust: Oxford University Press

Lelean, S R (1980a) Research in nursing: an overview of DHSS initiatives in developing research in nursing – 1. *Nursing Times Occasional Papers* **76**, 5–8

Lelean, S R (1980b) Research in nursing: an overview of DHSS initiatives in developing research in nursing – 2. *Nursing Times Occasional Papers* **76**, 9–12

Ley, P (1979) Memory for medical information. *British Journal of Social and Clinical Psychology* **18**, 245–255

Ley, P (1981) Professional non-compliance: a neglected problem. *British Journal of Clinical Psychology* **20**, 151–154

McFarlane, J K & Castledine, G (1982) *A Guide to the Practice of Nursing Using the Nursing Process* London: C V Mosby

Mook, D G (1982) *Psychological Research. Strategy and Tactics* New York: Harper and Row

Müller, D J (1980) Further thoughts on 'teaching psychology in health studies courses'. *Journal of Further and Higher Education* **4**, 52–55

Müller, D J (1981) Applied human science: is explanation enough? *British Journal of Medical Psychology* **54**, 287–288

Orr, J A (1979) Nursing and the process of scientific enquiry. *Journal of Advanced Nursing* **4**, 603–610

Roper, N, Logan, N W & Tierney, A J (1981) *Learning to Use the Process of Nursing* Edinburgh: Churchill Livingstone

Royal College of Nursing (1982) *Research-Mindedness and Nurse Education* London: Royal College of Nursing

Simpson, M (1971) Research in nursing: the first step. *Nursing Mirror* **132**, 22–27

Sommer, R & Sommer, B B (1980) *A Practical Guide to Behavioral Research* New York: Oxford University Press

Van Bree, N S (1981) Undergraduate research. *Nursing Outlook* **29**, 39–41

Wattley, L A (1982) Critical reading for nurses. *Nurse Education Today* **2**, 11–12

Wattley, L A & Müller, D J (1983a) Psychology and nursing: the case for an empirical approach. *Journal of Advanced Nursing* **8**, 107–110

Wattley, L A & Müller, D J 1983b) Towards a psychology of nursing. The authors reply. *Journal of Advanced Nursing* **8**, 341–342

CHAPTER 2

NURSES AS INDIVIDUALS

Nursing and psychology as we have seen are concerned with individuals and many nurses will be familiar with tutors insisting that patients be referred to by name to demonstrate a belief in their individuality and the need to preserve it. But it is not only patients who are of interest to psychologists. According to the British Psychological Society (1974) many nurses are unaware that psychology has anything to do with their own individual behaviour. It has also been suggested that '... knowing oneself is frequently a challenge unmet by nurses. We are so eager to focus on the behaviour and potentials of others that we too rarely seek self-appraisal.' (Reres 1974, p.671.) This chapter will concentrate on nurses themselves and on what factors may be associated with them wanting to become nurses. Are all nurses similar in personality? Are there characteristics and qualities which are needed in nursing and which should be identified to help in careers talks for school-leavers, or selection interviews for nursing? As Clark & Hockey (1979) point out, 'there has, historically, been an understandable concern that the "right" kind of person should be recruited into the nursing profession, both in the interests of the patients and in an attempt to reduce avoidable wastage to a minimum' (p.121).

Just exactly what is the right kind of person? Many nurses seem to feel that there is such a thing as a 'typical' nursing personality (Cooper *et al.* 1976). This suggests that anyone who becomes a nurse has some enduring personal characteristic(s) which is shared with most nurses. MacGuire (1969) puts it another way: 'for those who survive the basic training course personal identity is inextricably bound up with identity as a nurse' (p.107). This implies that the characteristics are acquired in training, rather than being present beforehand.

In studying people who become nurses a variety of factors have been taken into account by researchers. These include age, type of schooling, intellect, parental attitudes, number of previous occupations, job satisfaction and personality. There is a wide variety of studies which have focused on different groups of people: schoolchildren, potential nurses, nurses in training, qualified junior and senior nurses, nurses in specific fields such as psychiatry, and unqualified as well as qualified nurses no longer nursing. (For a detailed review see Birch 1975.) Many of these studies have concentrated on different research questions so they are not easy to compare. However, a great number has considered personality, a topic of particular interest to psychologists.

People use the word personality to describe the way people are perceived in relation to others. Their personality is the thing that distinguishes them from others: the strong-willed from the weak-willed; dominant from subordinate; extrovert from introvert. Psychologists have tried to define personality more precisely. One typical definition suggests it is 'the characteristic patterns of behaviour and modes of thinking that determine a person's adjustment to the environment' (Hilgard *et al.* 1979, p.377). Such a definition gives us the impression that personality tends to be an enduring factor which will not necessarily change according to the situation. Another view is that personality is in fact situationally determined (cf. Endler & Magnusson 1976). It is, however, generally agreed that personality can refer to intelligence, emotional and social qualities, interests, attitudes, motivation and temperament.

Caine (1964) has suggested that there are two distinct requirements for a good nurse: one is concerned with intellectual ability, the other with the ability to establish personal relations. Both of these can be seen as aspects of personality. Economic factors and problems associated with low standards of nursing care have created the need for an increased understanding of the qualities which lead to good nursing. However, those studies of nurses that have considered personality have not been able to determine what personality is associated with being a good nurse. Instead they have helped form pictures of the personalities of individuals and groups to compare nurses with other professions.

A personality questionnaire that has been used with nurses is Cattell's Sixteen Personality Factor Inventory (1957). The factors Cattell includes are meant to cover all the main areas of personality in which people can differ and an interesting account of how these were arrived at is provided by Kline (1981). The first British student nurses measured by his inventory (Cordiner 1968) were found to be above average in intelligence, sensitivity, seriousness, shyness and conservatism, but below average in self-control and emotional maturity. When Cordiner compared her results with those of American studies she found that there were differences. American student nurses were above average in emotional maturity and also in persistence. An important point about this study and others is that they did not investigate to what extent these personality types proved to be good or bad nurses.

Birch (1975) attempted to overcome this shortcoming by comparing the results of psychological tests including the Cattell Inventory with ratings of nurses' performance by ward sisters. This was not easy, but it showed that although there were personality differences between pupil and student nurses, there were no differences on such criteria as attitudes to patients, initiative and ability to work in a team. The sorts of differences that were suggested by the psychological tests portrayed student nurses as more intelligent, assertive, independent, aggressive and stubborn and the pupil nurses as more humble, mild, benevolent, conforming, persevering, emotionally mature, ordered and conscientious.

Singh & MacGuire (1971) suggested that the evidence points to the possibility that 'individuals in various occupations may be differentiated according to personality characteristics and personal values' (p.165). They discuss several studies which indicate that 'occupational choice is the result of perceived similarity of self and occupations' (p.165) and they cite Slegelman & Peek (1960) as suggesting that a person chooses a certain vocation because it has job requirements that satisfy his or her personal needs. This question of 'needs' had been used by Singh (1972) in a study of English nurses using the Edwards Personal Preference Schedule (1959). This test measures 'perceived needs' by presenting the subjects with a large number of statements and asking them to choose those which most represent how they feel. The test results when analysed give scores for 15 specific needs. For example, if you have the kind of personality which desires success you would score high on the need for 'Achievement'. Other needs measured include: 'Order' (the need to have things planned and organized); 'Autonomy' (the need to feel free to do as you wish, criticize authority); 'Nurturance' (the desire to encourage others, sympathize and be generous). Singh's study enabled him to draw up a profile of the typical English student nurse based on these perceived needs. He found that 'the needs most characteristic of this group of student nurses are high order, autonomy, nurturance, endurance, heterosexuality and aggression, and low achievement, dominance, exhibition and affiliation' (p.48). The reader is encouraged to read Singh's article for a full description of these needs and the profile of English student nurses obtained.

All the studies described so far concerned nurses who had already begun training. This means that when they took the tests they may already have responded to their nursing environment in certain ways which would affect the results. To overcome this problem some studies have tested students before their course started. They have been retested later in training when their performance as nurses could also be rated. Many of these studies were concerned with which nurses stayed in nursing, and which ones left (known as the 'wastage' problem). Wittmeyer et al. (1971) found that nurses who carried on with nursing rather than giving up were more adventurous and independent individuals. Singh & Smith (1975) suggest that a typical voluntary leaver may be someone who is 'unable or unwilling to put herself second to the requirements necessary to make a hospital function satisfactorily' (p.49). Another of their conclusions, inferred from the results of a Cattell Inventory, was that 'people who leave nurse training because they feel it is not for them (for whatever reason) appear to be too trusting and easy going and are probably the type of people who get involved with patients and are unable to retain the correct amount of detachedness necessary to be a successful nurse' (p.49). One difficulty with statements such as these is that they can imply the value judgement that a 'leaver' is a failure; this is unfortunate. As Clark (1977) has pointed out, it could be the institutions which are at fault.

There is still no clear evidence from these studies that a particular type of personality makes a good or bad nurse. Clarke has firmly criticized the pre-occupation with searching for an 'ideal personality' or the 'right person' for nursing, because it suggests that someone who does not succeed in nurse training is at fault. She suggests that there may be factors within hospitals or training schools which account for high wastage rates, but instead the individual nurse gets the blame if he or she apparently has the 'wrong' personality for nursing.

It is one thing to use personality information for recruitment and the prevention of wastage in nursing, but quite another to allow nurses to explore their own personalities with the help of psychological tests to increase self-awareness. It is this area which has been less well researched. Common sense tells us that there are all kinds of people working as nurses and that there is not an ideal type. It would be extremely dull if every nurse reading this book were exactly the same. On the other hand, to evaluate objectively our own decisions and the way we work with other people, it can be argued that it is important to know something about ourselves. If we are extroverted and quick tempered it is likely that we behave differently from the quiet introvert. This chapter gives you the opportunity to discover a little more about your own behaviour and to see how you compare with your colleagues.

Practical 2.1 A case study of oneself

Introduction

This practical is designed to enable you to explore different facets of your own personality and if you wish to compare your findings with those of your colleagues. We have selected four tests to help give you a greater understanding of the kind of person you are. We expect that within your group there will be a wide range of different personalities which we believe is of benefit to the nursing profession. Hence you should expect to find differences between yourselves, your peers and of course your tutors.

The first scale for you to complete is shown in Table 2.1. This is an American test designed by Fibel & Hale (1978) measuring your expectancy for success. This is defined as 'the expectancy held by an individual that in most situations he/she will be able to attain desired goals' (p.924) In Table 2.2 are a selection of questions taken from the Eysenck Personality Inventory (Eysenck & Eysenck 1964) a widely used British test of personality. These questions measure extroversion and introversion, that is the extent to which people are carefree, spontaneous, sociable, easy-going, etc., rather than quiet, retiring, serious individuals. The questions in Table 2.3 are samples of the kind of items included in a well known American test designed by Rotter (1966). These measure beliefs about internal and external control, that is the 'beliefs that rewards come from one's own behaviour or from external sources' (Rotter 1971, p.42). The final test shown in Table 2.4 concerns assertiveness. Its American creators, Gambrill & Richey (1975), designed it to measure the degree of discomfort felt in certain situations coupled with the likelihood of behaving in an assertive way in these same situations. They argue that there is an important relation between how a person feels and what a person does.

In completing these tests you will find it quite easy to fake your answers now that we have explained their content to you. This is of course up to you. However, whether you answer the questions truthfully or not, this practical will allow you to find out more about yourself, even if it is only the way in which you answer personal questions.

Table 2.1   Hale–Fibel Generalized Expectancy for Success Scale

Directions: Please indicate the degree to which you believe each statement would apply to you personally by circling the appropriate number, according to the following key:

1 = highly improbable
2 = improbable
3 = equally improbable and probable, not sure
4 = probable
5 = highly probable

In the future I expect that I will:	Number
1. find that people don't seem to understand what I am trying to say	1 2 3 4 5
2. be discouraged about my ability to gain the respect of others	1 2 3 4 5
3. be a good parent	1 2 3 4 5
4. be unable to accomplish my goals	1 2 3 4 5
5. have a successful marital relationship	1 2 3 4 5
6. deal poorly with emergency situations	1 2 3 4 5
7. find my efforts to change situations I don't like are ineffective	1 2 3 4 5
8. not be very good at learning new skills	1 2 3 4 5
9. carry through my responsibilities successfully	1 2 3 4 5
10. discover that the good in life outweighs the bad	1 2 3 4 5
11. handle unexpected problems successfully	1 2 3 4 5
12. get the promotions I deserve	1 2 3 4 5
13. succeed in the projects I undertake	1 2 3 4 5
14. not make any significant contributions to society	1 2 3 4 5
15. discover that my life is not getting much better	1 2 3 4 5
16. be listened to when I speak	1 2 3 4 5
17. discover that my plans don't work out too well	1 2 3 4 5
18. find that no matter how hard I try, things just don't turn out the way I would like	1 2 3 4 5
19. handle myself well whatever situation I'm in	1 2 3 4 5
20. be able to solve my own problems	1 2 3 4 5
21. succeed at most things I try	1 2 3 4 5
22. be successful in my endeavours in the long run	1 2 3 4 5
23. be very successful working out my personal life	1 2 3 4 5
24. experience many failures in my life	1 2 3 4 5
25. make a good first impression on people I meet for the first time	1 2 3 4 5
26. attain the career goals I have set for myself	1 2 3 4 5
27. have difficulty dealing with my superiors	1 2 3 4 5
28. have problems working with others	1 2 3 4 5
29. be a good judge of what it takes to get ahead	1 2 3 4 5
30. achieve recognition in my profession	1 2 3 4 5

Fibel, B & Hale, W D (1978) The Generalized Expectancy for Success Scale – a new measure. *Journal of Consulting and Clinical Psychology* **46**, 924–931. Copyright 1978 by the American Psychological Association. Reprinted by permission of the author.

Table 2.2 Scale measuring degree of extroversion–introversion

Instructions: Try to decide whether 'YES' or 'NO' represents your usual way of acting or feeling. Then put a cross under the heading 'YES' or 'NO'. Work quickly, and don't spend too much time over any question; we want your first reaction, not a long drawn-out thought process. The whole questionnaire shouldn't take more than a few minutes. Be sure not to omit any questions.

Question	YES	NO
1. Do you often long for excitement?		
2. Are you usually carefree?		
3. Do you stop and think things over before doing anything?		
4. Do you generally do and say things quickly without stopping to think?		
5. Would you do almost anything for a dare?		
6. Do you often do things on the spur of the moment?		
7. Generally, do you prefer reading to meeting people?		
8. Do you like going out a lot?		
9. Do you prefer to have few but special friends?		
10. When people shout at you do you shout back?		
11. Can you usually let yourself go and enjoy yourself a lot at a lively party?		
12. Do other people think of you as being very lively?		
13. Are you mostly quiet when you are with other people?		
14. If there is something you want to know about, would you rather look it up in a book than talk to someone about it?		
15. Do you like the kind of work that you need to pay close attention to?		
16. Do you hate being in a crowd who play jokes on one another?		
17. Do you like doing things in which you have to act quickly?		
18. Are you slow and unhurried in the way you move?		
19. Do you like talking to people so much that you never miss a chance of talking to a stranger?		
20. Would you be very unhappy if you could not see lots of people most of the time?		
21. Would you say that you are fairly self-confident?		
22. Do you find it hard to really enjoy yourself at a lively party?		
23. Can you easily get some life into a rather dull party?		
24. Do you like playing pranks on others?		

Eysenck, H J & Eysenck, S B G (1964) *Manual of the Eysenck Personality Inventory*. Reprinted with kind permission of the authors and the publishers Hodder and Stoughton.

Table 2.3 Scale measuring degree of internal–external control

I more strongly believe that:	Or
Promotions are earned through hard work and persistence	Making a lot of money is largely a matter of getting the right breaks
In my experience I have noticed that there is usually a direct connection between how hard I study and the grades I get	Many times the reactions of teachers seem haphazard to me
The number of divorces indicates that more and more people are not trying to make their marriages work	Marriage is largely a gamble
When I am right I can convince others	It is silly to think that one can really change another person's basic attitudes
In our society a man's future earning power is dependent upon his ability	Getting promoted is really a matter of being a little luckier than the next guy
If one knows how to deal with people they are really quite easily led	I have little influence over the way other people behave
In my case the grades I make are the results of my own efforts; luck has little or nothing to do with it	Sometimes I feel that I have little to do with the grades I get
People like me can change the course of world affairs if we make ourselves heard	It is only wishful thinking to believe that one can really influence what happens in society at large
I am the master of my fate	A great deal that happens to me is probably a matter of chance.
Getting along with people is a skill that must be practiced	It is almost impossible to figure out how to please some people.

Table 2.4 Assertion Inventory

Many people experience difficulty in handling interpersonal situations requiring them to assert themselves in some way, for example, turning down a request, asking a favour, giving someone a compliment, expressing disapproval or approval, etc. Please indicate your degree of discomfort or anxiety in the space provided before each situation listed below. Utilize the following scale to indicate degree of discomfort:

1 = none
2 = a little
3 = a fair amount
4 = much
5 = very much

Then, go over the list a second time and indicate after each item the probability or likelihood of your displaying the behaviour if actually presented with the situation.* For example, if you rarely apologize when you are at fault, you would mark a '4' after that item. Utilize the following scale to indicate response probability:

1 = always do it
2 = usually do it
3 = do it about half the time
4 = rarely do it
5 = never do it

*Note. It is important to cover your discomfort ratings (located in front of the items) while indicating response probability. Otherwise, one rating may contaminate the other and a realistic assessment of your behaviour is unlikely. To correct for this, place a piece of paper over your discomfort ratings while responding to the situations a second time for response probability.

Degree of discomfort	Situation	Response probability
_____	1. Turn down a request to borrow your car	_____
_____	2. Compliment a friend	_____
_____	3. Ask a favour of someone	_____
_____	4. Resist sales pressure	_____
_____	5. Apologize when you are at fault	_____
_____	6. Turn down a request for a meeting or date	_____
_____	7. Admit fear and request consideration	_____
_____	8. Tell a person you are intimately involved with when he/she says or does something that bothers you	_____
_____	9. Ask for a raise	_____
_____	10. Admit ignorance in some area	_____
_____	11. Turn down a request to borrow money	_____
_____	12. Ask personal questions	_____

Degree of discomfort	Situation	Response probability
_____	13. Turn off a talkative friend	_____
_____	14. Ask for constructive criticism	_____
_____	15. Initiate a conversation with a stranger	_____
_____	16. Compliment a person you are romantically involved with or interested in	_____
_____	17. Request a meeting or a date with a person	_____
_____	18. Your initial request for a meeting is turned down and you ask the person again at a later time	_____
_____	19. Admit confusion about a point under discussion and ask for clarification	_____
_____	20. Apply for a job	_____
_____	21. Ask whether you have offended someone	_____
_____	22. Tell someone that you like them	_____
_____	23. Request expected service when such is not forthcoming, e.g. in a restaurant	_____
_____	24. Discuss openly with the person his/her criticism of your behaviour	_____
_____	25. Return defective items, e.g. store or restaurant	_____
_____	26. Express an opinion that differs from that of the person you are talking to	_____
_____	27. Resist sexual overtures when you are not interested	_____
_____	28. Tell the person when you feel he/she has done something that is unfair to you	_____
_____	29. Accept a date	_____
_____	30. Tell someone good news about yourself	_____
_____	31. Resist pressure to drink	_____
_____	32. Resist a significant person's unfair demand	_____
_____	33. Quit a job	_____
_____	34. Resist pressure to 'turn on'	_____
_____	35. Discuss openly with the person his/her criticism of your work	_____
_____	36. Request the return of borrowed items	_____
_____	37. Receive compliments	_____
_____	38. Continue to converse with someone who disagrees with you	_____
_____	39. Tell a friend or someone with whom you work when he/she says or does something that bothers you	_____
_____	40. Ask a person who is annoying you in a public situation to stop	_____

Gambrill, E D & Richey, C A (1975) An assertion inventory for use in assessment and research. *Behaviour Therapy* 6, 550–561. Reprinted with kind permission of the author and the publishers Academic Press.

Method

The tests for this practical can be found between pages 19 and 23. Do work quite quickly in completing them and be sure to answer each question. We completed this practical, including the scoring, with a group of 22 second-year SRN students in just over an hour. All our subjects were women. You may find it better to allow yourself slightly longer so you have more time for discussion of the results with your colleagues.

Results

The scoring keys for all four tests can be found in Appendix II along with guidelines to help you interpret the results. In Table 2.5 we have included the information collected from our own students and you can use this to help you interpret your own results. As you can see from the Table, you can either build up profiles of selected individuals by reading the Table across from left to right, or you can investigate the range of scores for each personality measure included.

In examining individual profiles it can be seen, for example, that the most introverted subject (subject no.3) scores quite low on the success scale, believes in a mixture of internal and external control, experiences great discomfort in being assertive but scores in the middle on the scale which measures her probability of responding in an assertive way. The subject most likely to respond in situations requiring assertiveness (subject no.9) still experiences considerable discomfort, but has a particularly high belief in being successful. You may find it interesting to compare your individual profile with other members of your group.

In considering the scores for each personality measure it is enlightening to look at the average score and the range of scores. From our results the range of scores on the success scale is from 84 to 138 and the average score is 106.3 (2338/22). There is a wide range of scores on the measure of extroversion, from 9 to 19 and the average score is 14.1 (310/22). For the internal–external control scale, eight nurses had I scores, seven had neither I nor E scores and seven had E scores. The most frequent combination was 5 I with 5 E which we scored as 0 (see Scoring key in Appendix II), although there was a wide range of scores from 8 I to 6 E. For the measure of discomfort there was a range from 72 to 145 and an average score of 99.5 (2190/22). There was also a wide range of scores for the measure of probability, from 89 to 152 with an average score of 113.8 (2504/22). It will be interesting for you to compare your group scores with the results from our subjects.

Table 2.5 Personality scores for a group of second-year student nurses

Subject no.	Success scale	Extroversion–introversion	Internal–external	Assertiveness Discomfort	Probability
1	96	20	4E	122	152
2	106	16	0	102	108
3	99	9	0	135	114
4	98	14	6E	79	113
5	105	11	2I	105	120
6	96	12	0	106	105
7	84	11	0	76	114
8	99	11	2I	98	120
9	131	16	0	99	89
10	138	13	2I	112	108
11	112	13	2I	85	109
12	99	18	4I	105	109
13	86	18	0	145	116
14	96	13	0	79	111
15	109	17	2E	76	116
16	118	14	6I	72	132
17	124	15	8I	95	107
18	102	15	2E	99	115
19	111	14	4E	92	110
20	109	14	4E	101	104
21	106	19	2E	111	118
22	114	17	6I	96	114

Discussion

As we predicted in the introduction to this practical we found considerable individual differences in our group of nurses. It is clear from these data that there is not such a thing as a 'typical' nursing personality, the individual variation is too great. Nor is it clear from these kind of data whether on the basis of such tests one could select nurses who have the necessary skills to establish good personal relations. With the information we have it would seem extremely unlikely.

It is, however, interesting to use this information to compare groups of nurses with themselves and with other groups of people. For example, our subjects were tested in two self-selected groups, subjects nos 1–11 and 12–22, and we noticed that the second group was clearly more extroverted. This was in fact the case: subjects nos 1–11 scored an average of 12.4 on the extroversion scale, whereas the other group scored an average of 15.8. In this instance it would seem that the nurses may have grouped themselves according to some facet of personality.

In comparing the scores of our nurses with other groups of people a number of interesting conclusions can be drawn. The average score on the scale measuring belief in future success is slightly below that of the American sample, although the range for our group of women nurses is more like that of men rather than women undergraduates. For extroversion the average score for our group is particularly high, although our small sample may have distorted the results. The average score for degree of predicted discomfort was almost the same as that for the American sample, although the average response probability score was slightly higher. There are no norms available for this particular scale measuring the degree of internal and external control.

You may find it interesting as another practical to test other groups of subjects to see if you can find any differences between them and yourselves. The data from this practical suggest that, although you might find small differences between groups, you are more likely to find greater variation within groups.

Conclusion

In this chapter we have given you the opportunity to discover a bit more about yourself. We believe that this is a good way to use personality tests especially with subjects who have chosen careers which involve close contact with people. As Bannister (1982) argues,

> To try and understand oneself is not simply an interesting pastime, it is a necessity of life. In order to plan our future and to make choices we have to be able to anticipate our behaviour in future situations. This makes self-knowledge a practical guide, not a self-indulgence.
> (p.68).

We support this argument and believe the search for the 'ideal' nursing personality to be misguided. It is our view that nurses need to know themselves to become aware of how they as individuals can best develop the personal skills necessary for effective nursing. The fact that nursing like other professions attracts a wide range of individuals should be seen as a strength rather than as a weakness.

Summary

In this chapter we have presented four tests for measuring different facets of personality for the reader to complete. We have discussed whether there is such a thing as a 'typical' nursing personality and from the results of the practical have suggested that there is not. Instead, we have argued that it is more important that nurses have the opportunity to learn about the kind of people they are, to further their understanding of how they can learn to work with others.

References

Bannister, D (1982) Knowledge of self. In J. Hall (ed.) *Psychology for Nurses and Health Visitors* Leicester/London: The British Psychological Society/Macmillan Press

Birch J (1975) *To Nurse or Not to Nurse* London: Royal College of Nursing

British Psychological Society (1974) Teaching psychology to nurses. *Bulletin of the British Psychological Society* **27**, 272–283

Caine, T (1964) Personality tests for nurses. *Nursing Times* **60**, 973–974

Cattell, R B (1957) *16 Personality Factor Questionnaire* Champaign, Illinois: The Institute for Personality and Ability

Clark, J & Hockey, L (1979) *Research for Nursing – A Guide for the Enquiring Nurse* Aylesbury: HM & M

Clark, M (1977) Research in nurse education. *Nursing Times Occasional Papers* 17 February, 25–28

Cooper, C L, Lewis, B L & Moores, B (1976) Personality profiles of long serving senior nurses: implications for recruitment and selection. *International Journal of Nursing Studies* **13**, 251–257

Cordiner, C M (1968) Personality testing of Aberdeen student nurses. *Nursing Times* **64**, 178–180

Edwards, A L 1959) *Manual for the Edwards Personal Preference Schedule* New York: Psychological Corporation

Endler, N S & Magnusson, D (1976) *Interactional Psychology and Personality* Washington: Hemisphere

Eysenck, H J & Eysenck, S B G (1964) *Manual of the Eysenck Personality Inventory* Sevenoaks: Hodder and Stoughton

Fibel, B & Hale, W. D. (1978) The Generalized Expectancy for Success Scale – a new measure. *Journal of Consulting and Clinical Psychology* **45**, 924–931

Gambrill, E D & Richey, C A (1975) An assertion inventory for use in assessment and research. *Behavior Therapy* **6**, 550–561

Hilgard, E R, Atkinson, R L & Atkinson, R C (1979) *Introduction to Psychology* 7th edn. New York: Harcourt, Brace, Jovanovich

Kline, P (1981) The work of Eysenck and Cattell. In F. Fransella (ed.) *Personality* London: Methuen.

MacGuire, J (1969) Threshold to nursing. Occasional Papers on Social Administration, no. 30. London: Bell and Sons

Reres, M (1974) Assessing growth potential. *American Journal of Nursing* **74**, 670–676

Rotter, J B (1966) Generalized expectancies for internal versus external control of reinforcement. *Psychological Monographs* **80** (whole no. 609)

Rotter, J B (1971) External control and internal control. *Psychology Today* 37–42, 58–59

Singh, A (1972) Personality needs of an English sample of student nurses. *Nursing Times Occasional Papers* 23 March, 47–48

Singh, A & MacGuire, J (1971) Occupational values and stereotypes in a group of trained nurses. *Nursing Times Occasional Papers* 21 October, 165–168

Singh, A & Smith, J (1975) Retention and withdrawal of student nurses. *International Journal of Nursing Studies* **12**, 43–56

Slegelman, M & Peek, R F (1960) Personality patterns related to occupational roles. *Genetic Psychology Monographs* **619**, 291–305 (Cited in Singh & MacGuire 1971, *op. cit.*)

Wittmeyer, A L, Camiscioni, J S & Purdy, P A (1971) A longitudinal study of attrition and academic performance in a collegiate nursing program for nursing candidates. *Nursing Research* **20**, 339–347

CHAPTER 3

LIFE EVENTS IN ILLNESS AND HEALTH

Research related to life events has become an area of increasing interest to psychologists and to those professions specializing in the care of others. Throughout our lives we are subject to a number of specific events which by their nature impose change on our ways of behaving. We may move house, start a new job, study for a qualification, get married, have children, gain promotion or experience any number of events which have positive effects on our lives. Similarly there are an unfortunately large number of events which have negative effects: the death of a close family member, entering hospital as a patient, marital separation, being unhappy at work and so forth. What all these events have in common is that they require significant changes in the lifestyle of those individuals affected. Such events whether positive or negative are clearly stressful and it is necessary for individuals to learn to cope with the new demands being placed on them. From the perspective it is possible to investigate life-span development (from birth through old age) in terms of how individuals experience and adjust to the inevitable series of stressful life events which befall them.

Holmes & Rahe (1967) first attempted to define the types of life events which produce stress and began to investigate how these might contribute to ill-health. A list of 43 life events derived from their own clinical experience was compiled and presented to a large sample of subjects. They were told that marriage was to be given an arbitrary value of 500 points and that they should indicate for each life event whether they thought it required more or less readjusting to than their marriage. Having decided this they were then asked to choose a proportionately larger or smaller number for each life event to give a comparative value with marriage. These scores were then scaled so that the life event rated most significant was awarded 100 points. The full Social Readjustment Rating Scale can be seen in Table 3.1. To arrive at a 'Life Change Score' you need only indicate whether or not each event has happened to you over the last year and add up the total of values. This gives a tentative indication of the likelihood of future ill-health. It is suggested that of those people with over 300 Life Change Units almost 80% get ill in the near future. Of those with 150–299 Units, about 50% get ill and with less than 150 only about 30% get ill.

Another method of obtaining similar information has been used by Brown & Harris (1978) in their study of depression. They used a semi-structured interview to obtain a more thorough understanding of the interpretation placed on events by different people. Parry et al. (1981) have reported on the high reliability of this approach as compared with the general use of a checklist.

It is still unclear exactly what effects major life events have on physical and psychiatric well-being. In a book edited by Gunderson & Rahe (1974) a number of studies are reported tracing the links between life stress and illness. Steptoe (1981), in a detailed review of psychological factors in cardiovascular disorders, suggests that major life events do appear to have a significant effect. He also notes that there is a correlation between bereavement and cardiovascular death. Similarly, Cooper (1982) has argued that the study of life events in the pathogenesis of cancer is potentially a very fruitful field for future research, despite some of the difficulties involved in measuring them. In a general review paper set more in a nursing context Miller (1981) emphasizes the need for more sensitive measures before any definite conclusions can be drawn. He does, however, suggest that:

'The scientific community must appreciate efforts made so far to identify and analyse the impact of life events on psychological and physical adjustment'.
(p.320)

From the point of view of nursing this relation is important. A number of the life events identified by Holmes & Rahe (1967) are the concern of the nurse. Major personal injury or illness is very high on the list, as is pregnancy. The effect of bereavement on family members also scores very high and here the nurse may be expected to provide some support and comfort. But perhaps it is the large number of less highly rated events such as changes in eating habits which are often the direct result of ill-

Table 3.1 Social Readjustment Rating Scale

Life event	Value
1. Death of spouse	100
2. Divorce	73
3. Marital separation from mate	65
4. Detention in jail or other institution	63
5. Death of a close family member	63
6. Major personal injury or illness	53
7. Marriage	50
8. Being fired at work	47
9. Marital reconciliation with mate	45
10. Retirement from work	45
11. Major change in the health or behaviour of a family member	44
12. Pregnancy	40
13. Sexual difficulties	39
14. Gaining a new family member (e.g. through birth, adoption, oldster moving in, etc.)	39
15. Major business readjustment (e.g. merger, reorganization, bankruptcy, etc.)	39
16. Major change in financial state (e.g. a lot worse off or a lot better off than usual)	38
17. Death of a close friend	37
18. Changing to a different line of work	36
19. Major change in the number of arguments with spouse (e.g. either a lot more or a lot less than usual regarding child-rearing, personal habits, etc.)	35
20. Taking out a mortgage or loan for a major purchase (e.g. for a home, business, etc.)	31
21. Foreclosure on a mortgage or loan	30
22. Major change in responsibilities at work (e.g. promotion, demotion, lateral transfer)	29
23. Son or daughter leaving home (e.g. marriage, attending college, etc.)	29
24. Trouble with in-laws	29
25. Outstanding personal achievement	28
26. Wife beginning or ceasing work outside the home	26
27. Beginning or ceasing formal schooling	26
28. Major change in living conditions (e.g. building a new home, remodelling, deterioration of home or neighbourhood)	25
29. Revision of personal habits (dress, manners, association, etc.)	24
30. Troubles with the boss	23
31. Major change in working hours or conditions	20
32. Change in residence	20
33. Changing to a new school	20
34. Major change in usual type and/or amount of recreation	19
35. Major change in church activities (e.g. a lot more or a lot less than usual)	19

Life event	Value
36. Major change in social activities (e.g. clubs, dancing, movies, visiting, etc.)	18
37. Taking out a mortgage or loan for a lesser purchase (e.g. for a car, TV, freezer, etc.)	17
38. Major change in sleeping habits (a lot more or a lot less sleep or change in part of day when asleep)	16
39. Major change in number of family get-togethers (e.g. a lot more or a lot less than usual)	15
40. Major change in eating habits (a lot more or a lot less food intake, or very different meal hours or surroundings)	15
41. Vacation	13
42. Christmas	12
43. Minor violations of the law (e.g. traffic tickets, jaywalking, disturbing the peace, etc.)	11

Holmes, T H & Rahe, R H (1967) The Social Readjustment Rating Scale. *Journal of Psychosomatic Research* **11**, 213–218. Reprinted with kind permission of the authors and the publishers Pergamon.

ness that contribute more to our understanding of the needs of patients. Many illnesses do require personal change, perhaps to a different line of work or to different social activities for example. It may be the cumulative effect of events such as these that most affect a patient's recovery or motivation to get well.

This chapter enables the reader to investigate a number of common life events from a developmental perspective. Although the emphasis is on methodology, specifically interviewing, the design of questionnaires and content analysis, it is hoped that this chapter will serve as a general introduction to the topic of life-span development, from birth through old age.

Practical 3.1 An investigation into the experience of becoming a parent

Introduction

Table 3.1 indicates that pregnancy and gaining a new family member constitute major life events. Several other factors from the list may also be associated with these life events, such as whether or not the mother ceases to work, a change in residence or a change in social activities. It is unlikely that different individuals will experience becoming a parent in exactly the same way and often the best way to find out how parents view this new experience is to interview them.

Asking questions is often a part of a nurse's work in collecting information from patients. Sometimes this is a simple matter of asking for a name or address, but sometimes it is more difficult because of the personal or emotional nature of the topic, as for example with pain, fear or discomfort. Some research suggests that nurses tend to limit the conversations they have with patients to technical rather than emotional matters (Clark 1981). In this practical we are going to discover how to incorporate questions into an interview schedule and how to carry it out. Interviews are means of discovering 'in depth' information which might be difficult to obtain using other procedures. As Lewin (1979) notes, 'whereas observation permits us to see behaviour in action, interviewing permits us to understand how people feel about things and how they perceive their world' (p.228).

Before describing how to carry out the practical we will examine the topic chosen for investigation, becoming a parent, in more detail. This will provide the background material for the practical.

Becoming a parent

What is it like to become a parent? Does being a mother or father come naturally? Do prospective parents know what to expect when they add children to their family unit? There seem to be all sorts of possible reasons for chosing parenthood. In an American study on the value of children to parents Hoffman & Hoffman (1973) investigated factors such as confirmation of one's status as an adult, the sense of making a contribution to the group or community, extending the sources of affection and loving ties and stimulation, novelty and fun. One can also think of cultures in which children are regarded as important and necessary contributors to the family income.

Deciding to have a child for any particular reason does not necessarily mean that parenting is always a rewarding experience. Rapoport & Rapoport (1977) point out that being a parent creates as well as interferes with life opportunities and a study by Hoffman & Manis (1978) demonstrates the existence of positive and negative responses by both parents. Examples of positive responses include feeling more mature and stable, having a family feeling and increase of love, happiness and sense of achievement. Examples of negative responses include feeling tied down, losing one's individuality, feeling life is no longer one's own and experiencing an increase of work, money problems and worries.

A study by Oakley (1980) found that first-time mothers presented a surprisingly negative picture of the early experience of parenting. According to Oakley many of the mothers in her sample described the experience as one of shock. Although they had really looked forward to being 'promoted' to motherhood, they were disappointed by the reality of having an infant to cope with. A frequent question they continued to ask was why don't they tell you it will be like this, referring to sleepless nights, exhaustion, discomfort and insecurity. Many complained that the various baby books and medical authorities failed to describe parenthood as it really is.

The outcomes of Oakley's study related to three main areas: the mental health of the mothers postdelivery, feelings of satisfaction with motherhood and feelings for the baby. In her study only two out of the 55 studied experienced no negative mental-health effect in the transition to motherhood. Four-fifths experienced 'the blues' (short-term reaction to the birth), three-quarters experienced anxiety (heightened state of anxiety on first being alone with and responsible for the baby), one-third experienced 'depressed mood' (fluctuating condition in early motherhood) and one-quarter experienced depression (more disabling, clinically definable depression which interferes with physical well-being and coping). In terms of satisfaction with motherhood, one-third of the mothers had less than 'high' satisfaction with their role, and in terms of feelings for the baby at 5 months postdelivery, two-thirds had less than 'good' feelings.

Oakley related these outcomes to various factors and these are summarized briefly in Table 3.2. She found that the effects of 'vulnerability' factors such as bad housing and lack of maternal control are cumulative. Thus the risk of depression, for example, was found to increase with the number of factors experienced by the mothers. One reason why Oakley presents a more negative picture than Hoffman & Manis may be that her study concentrated on very new first-time mothers up to 5 months postdelivery, whereas theirs involved parents with older children, who may have modified their views with increasing experience and success in raising offspring.

Oakley argues that 'childbirth is a life event akin to others' (p.179). Although one might think of pregnancy and the birth of a first child as a

Table 3.2 Summary of findings from Oakley's (1980) study

Outcome	Related factors
Postnatal blues	Instrumental delivery, epidural, dissatisfaction with 2nd stage of labour
Depression	Technological birth, lack of maternal control, dissatisfaction with birth management, little or no previous contact with babies
Depressed mood	Bad housing, lack of help from father, lack of employment outside the home
Anxiety	Not related to birth as such, but to first-time motherhood
Satisfaction with motherhood	Capacity to view self as a mother and feelings about feminine role
Feelings for baby	Feelings about feminine role, baby's sex and sleeping habits, current life situation (housing, no employment, missing work, lack of help from father).

Adapted from Oakley, A (1980) *Women Confined: Towards a Sociology of Childbirth* p.143. Printed with kind permission of the author and the publishers Martin Robertson.

positive life event associated with all sorts of gain (adult status, parenthood, status as a family), Oakley found elements of loss involved which were important enough in some women to lead to depression in some form. She states that 'life events constitute loss events if their major effect is to deprive a person of sources of value or reward' (p.251).

We now have a picture of various reactions which people may experience in response to life events associated with becoming parents. The practical that follows will enable students to devise questions to help them understand a person's response to one or more aspects of becoming a parent. Oakley tried to compare the expectations of mothers about pregnancy, birth and early parenthood with their experience of reality.

Method

The aim of this practical is to design and carry out an interview schedule on a mother known to the student who has relatively recent experience of parenthood. This practical can be carried out by individuals or small groups in the class, although it is desirable for each participant to carry out an actual interview even if small groups design one schedule between them. The diploma in nursing students who carried out this practical either did the whole project alone or discussed the design of the interview together, and then interviewed a subject individually, thus providing results which they could compare. The purpose of the interview is to identify both the expectations of parenthood as held by the subject and the reality which was experienced.

The use of interviews requires considerable expertise both in terms of design and administration. There are a number of general points which need to be considered and the following notes are designed to help you.

1. Interviews can either be highly structured, that is tightly controlled by the interviewer, or relatively unstructured. Loosely structured interviews allow the interviewer a greater degree of flexibility but may make interviewing itself more difficult. Furthermore the analysis of results may be more difficult.

2. It is preferable to try out the interview schedule by doing a pilot study to check that the questions are meaningful and elicit appropriate answers. The interviewer should also be sure that all the topics which need to be covered are included in the schedule.

3. Extreme care must be taken in designing questions. They must be clear, unambiguous and of a suitable level for the subject. Furthermore interviewer bias must be avoided. It is very easy to design questions that reflect the presenter's own biases.

4. Consideration should also be given to the ordering of questions. It may pay to move from broad open questions to relatively closed questions requiring specific information, or vice versa.

5. To collect more 'in-depth' information probes might need to be used. These are questions specifically inserted to try and get more detailed information often about more sensitive topics. If such probes are threatening or challenging it may be best to incorporate them late in the interview.

6. It is advisable to use a tape-recorder in order that one has a permanent record of the interview. Even more appropriate is to record the interview on video which enables non-verbal behaviour to be analysed in some detail.

7. Finally, some initial consideration should be given to how the data, once collected, are to be analysed.

There are a number of useful guides to interviewing and students can refer as appropriate to Lewin (1979) or Sommer & Sommer (1980). In an extremely detailed text Moser & Kalton (1971) present a comprehensive description of how to carry out large-scale survey interviews.

Having designed the interview each participant should find one person who has had a child fairly recently. If necessary a person with more than one child could be asked to recall their first pregnancy, though some detail and accuracy may be lost. Interviewing someone about the experience of becoming a parent for the first time makes it easier for you to compare your findings with those of Oakley. The person selected should not be a patient but friends, work colleagues or social acquaintances could be approached. Our students all found friends who were willing to participate. Having found a subject, the interview should be arranged at a convenient time and place, perhaps the subject's home. Distractions should be minimized and a tape-recorder if acceptable may aid the process considerably since the interview schedule encourages rather discursive replies.

Results and discussion

The main purpose of this practical is to learn how to devise suitable interview questions and, more importantly, to help in the acquisition of the skills involved in carrying out an interview. Our students were able to compare their findings with those of Oakley and to note areas of similarity and of contrast. Rather than give a consensus of results, we have decided to include extracts from various interviews to illustrate varieties of questions and some of the answers given to them. These may give you ideas for constructing your own interview.

Many students initially asked for facts about family matters. This provided background information and prepared the subject for the more personal and pertinent questions to follow. The first few questions therefore included details such as age of interviewee and partner, marital status, type of accommodation, career or current employment, nationality, educational and family background and age of infant(s). This was recorded anonymously to maintain confidentiality.

The following question–answer extract shows how a student then built up a picture of what the mother expected pregnancy and the delivery to be like and of how prepared she might be for being a parent. The questions also focused on what pregnancy and the delivery were actually like and how the mother felt in the early months of being a mother.

Q. Was the pregnancy normal, or were any problems encountered?
A. The pregnancy was normal apart from morning sickness; with me,

however, it wasn't confined to the mornings. I started to be ill when I was about 5½ months pregnant and continued. I really didn't expect to be sick all the time.

Q. Had you any previous experience with babies?

A. The only experience was gained from work. As a student nurse I worked on both a children's ward and the obstetric unit. This really helped.

Q. Did you feel the actual childbirth was normal?

A. The childbirth was normal apart from my waters being broken. I did ask if they would do an episiotomy as I felt I was tearing but was told I didn't need one.

Q. Was it as you expected?

A. Not really. I didn't expect so much pain. Analgesia was offered but I was only able to have one dose as the baby was born quite quickly.

Q. Can you remember the feelings you felt once you held the babe?

A. I was relieved it was all over, but I felt really proud. I didn't feel maternal I was too tired. I just wanted to go to sleep, but I still wanted to hold her. I suppose my feelings were mixed, maybe if she'd been born during the day and I'd been able to rest I might have felt more maternal earlier.

Q. Did you have any preference as to the sex of your child and if so were you lucky?

A. No, we were unlucky, we both wanted a boy. I wasn't upset for too long but it took my husband longer to adjust.

Q. Were you at all depressed after the birth?

A. I didn't have any depression at all, in fact I was waiting for it to arrive: it never did. The only time I felt low was when I got home. I never realized a baby took up so much time.

This short extract demonstrates the value of questions which encourage the subject to say more than yes or no. The first question is especially true of this since the subject is able to describe the abnormality of her continuous sickness even though she says her pregnancy was normal. The subject clearly shows how reality differed from expectation in terms of pain, depression and the sex of the child. Two of these, pain and the child's sex, reflect Oakley's findings, but the third is in complete contrast.

It might seem more economical to collect the same sort of information using multiple-choice responses. One would, for example, list problems that can be encountered in pregnancy and ask the mother to check any which had affected her. However, it is very easy to exclude some responses which subjects may have experienced. Although it is easier to analyse data collected in this way, unless the choices are thoroughly prepared one risks overlooking information which may be important. This is one way in which a pilot study can sometimes indicate shortcomings before the main study and suggest whether an interview is the most appropriate technique. The next extract illustrates how two questions on the same subject differentiate between expectation before an event and the reality of it.

Q. Did you want your husband present during labour?
A. Yes.
Q. Do you think your husband's presence at the birth of your child helped you cope?
A. Well it was nice that he was there and I'm glad he was there but I can't stand any fuss. He kept on asking how I was, in the end I told him to be quiet.

The final extract demonstrates the use of probe questions to draw out information more clearly. It reads rather like a naturally occurring conversation and demonstrates a clear move from general topics to the subject's specific and personal experience.

Q. Were you told or shown anything about birth during your pregnancy?
A. Yes lots.
Q. (probe) What sort of things and can you remember who told you and where?
A. Well, for a start I've got a great GP and he gave me lots of encouragement about attending antenatal clinics and everything but mainly the doctors, and in particular the nurses, at the clinic told me and showed me a film about pregnancy and birth with all the stages of labour.
Q. (probe) Did they ever describe labour itself?
A. Yes, they just said it was contractions at intervals lessening in distance between until the birth. Mind you they never actually said it would hurt or anything. I suppose they should.
Q. (probe) Did you find that it did?
A. Oh yes like hell. Yes they should say.

The same student probed effectively at a later stage in the interview.

Q. Can you think of anything you wish you had not been told or shown about birth before you gave birth yourself?
A. Only the horror stories. I mean you've got to know the risks haven't you, and they aren't really all that great if you're healthy and careful, and they do tend to spot a lot now quite early on don't they?
Q. (probe) What do you mean by horror stories?
A. Well all the stories other mums tell you about ghastly births and practically week-long labours and everything. I mean you can do without that. Luckily there are always the others at clinics that reassure you with glowing tales of easy births. That's all though. I don't think there's anything else.

These extracts demonstrate some difference between expectation and reality in terms of pregnancy, birth and early parenthood. There may be as many different points of view about expectation and reality as there are people interviewed so it can be useful to compare findings in discussion with others. The interviews reveal the perceptions of the subjects about an important series of life events; it is interesting to record that several of the students were quite amazed at the feelings and experiences expressed in the interviews by friends with children. This is interesting as it suggests perhaps that professional experience had not enabled them to predict the feelings of people becoming parents.

In doing this practical some students felt it was difficult to interview someone about such a personal matter. An interview schedule needs to be designed thoughtfully and may take some time to prepare if it is not to cause offence or embarrassment. There is a fine line between encouraging the subject to divulge what they would like to and prying into an essentially private event.

Practical 3.2 Investigating life events: the questionnaire approach

Introduction

We have already discussed the wide range of events, both positive and negative, that can affect us throughout our lives. Any change in our patterns of behaviour or in our life-style are potentially threatening and have to be adjusted to. An interesting study of people's feelings at different ages was undertaken by Nicholson (1980) and reported in his book *Seven Ages*. These seven ages cover childhood, adolescence, young adulthood, parenthood, early middle-age, later middle-age and the retirement years. In this fascinating account of his research he suggests that people are not burdened by their age but develop and change as a result of major events many of which they wish on themselves.

For this practical we would like you to focus on a major event in the life-cycle which is typical of young adulthood, parenthood or early middle-age and to design a questionnaire to investigate it in more depth. It should be remembered that we all attach different degrees of importance to certain events and what is major to one person might be of little importance to somebody else. This doesn't matter and you should pick a topic which particularly interests you.

In Nicholson's survey young adulthood was considered to be between the ages of 17 and 25 years. This period culminates in the forming of an intimate relation which usually results in marriage. The period itself is seen as one of freedom and experimentation to 'find yourself'. The next period of early adulthood is assumed to begin with the birth of the first child. It stretches approximately between the ages of 26 and 38 years and is a period of family consolidation. Early middle-age, between the ages 39 and 48 years, is a time for looking ahead and planning for a life with less responsibility as children become more independent and elderly parents are no longer present. All these periods can be characterized by a number of similar events and you may want to concentrate on one of these. On the other hand, you may want to consider a more individual event which has particularly affected you.

Method

For this practical we want you to design a questionnaire to collect information about a life event. A great deal of research is carried out with questionnaires. It is a very productive technique but one which does need careful planning and preparation. Sommer & Sommer (1980) provide a good introduction to this topic. There is also an excellent chapter by Slater (1982) that takes students step by step through the design and implementation of a questionnaire. As in designing an interview schedule there are a number of points which must be considered.

1. It is important that the topic selected is suitable for investigating with a questionnaire. In particular, care should be taken not to select too broad a topic so as to make the questionnaire unmanageable.
2. Questions must of course be worded very carefully and be at a suitable level of understanding for the subjects.
3. Similarly ambiguous questions should be avoided, for example 'how do you feel?'.
4. Avoid double negatives such as, 'Are you against not having visitors on weekdays between 4 and 5 p.m.?'.
5. Do not include double-barrelled questions such as 'Cancer is a life-threatening illness; therefore more research into its causes should be our highest priority'. Respondents may not agree with both parts of the statement and if they agree with the first statement they may feel they have to go along with the second part.
6. As is the case for an interview, you will have to decide whether to use open or closed questions. Closed questions are usually more appropriate for questionnaires although you should invite your respondents to comment more broadly, possibly at the end.

7. Do pay careful attention to the design of your questionnaire especially the layout. Consideration must be given to the number of questions and their sequence. You should aim for a natural logical sequence which will elicit the information you seek. Make sure that the questionnaire is easy to follow and to fill in and that respondents are clear about what they have to do.

8. There is a clear difference between factual and evaluative questions. If it is your intention to elicit attitudes, special attention should be given to the use of suitable scaling techniques (see Practical 4.3).

9. The analysis of questionnaire data depends on the nature of the responses collected. Do give careful consideration to this in the design of your questionnaire. Think carefully about the kind of information you want to get and the ways in which you wish to present it once collected.

We undertook this practical with our group of diploma in nursing students. They divided into small groups and worked on designing a questionnaire which they were going to give to the remainder of the class. This worked quite well and avoided the problem of finding subjects. However, it might be more interesting for each group member to get the questionnaire filled in by say six subjects to get a better cross-section of the public.

Results and discussion

Our students selected a range of topics to investigate, including nurses' reasons for leaving the parental home and factors affecting choosing between public and private education. Of particular interest was a questionnaire designed to explore the attitudes of students towards the Diploma in Nursing course, which they had chosen to undertake. Clearly, for our group of students this was an important life event which had resulted in considerable changes to their lives. In many cases families were affected and in all cases the students had to adjust to allow themselves more study time. It is also likely that such a course once completed will change an individual's view of the world and make the person feel different in some way.

From this questionnaire it was found that 80% of the students felt that the course was interfering with their outside interests and activities. But what was very interesting was that 85% thought that work load was as expected, although the major source of anxiety was the volume of work

(Figure 3.1). Concern was also expressed about the thought of examinations and to a lesser extent handing in work on time. This suggests that the course members had a fairly realistic view of what the course would entail. It was also found that the main reasons for undertaking the course were to further their careers and to gain knowledge. This can be seen from the histogram in Figure 3.2. Rather surprisingly, financial gain was not seen as a major motivational factor, despite the feeling that career opportunities would be enhanced by taking the course. The information gathered from this questionnaire was clearly of relevance to the course members and of particular interest to prospective students of the Diploma in Nursing course.

Questionnaires can be extremely useful research tools and have often been used in nursing research. For example, Birch (1975) used a short questionnaire with yes/no responses to investigate nurses' attitudes toward various aspects of their training. Murray (1983) used one in an investigation of nurses' smoking behaviour and Nichols et al. (1981) made use of a questionnaire in a study concerned with job satisfaction among nurses. However, designing questionnaires requires practice and it is always worth trying out your draft questions on colleagues or friends and running pilot studies to iron out problems such as ambiguity. This not only enhances the credibility of your questionnaire with your subjects, but also facilitates the analysis of results.

So far in this chapter our practicals have involved us in obtaining the co-operation of subjects in the study of life events. However, there is a form of social research which can be done without any personal contact with subjects which will be the focus of the next practical.

Practical 3.3 An investigation concerning papers relating to the elderly in a nursing journal

Introduction

It is notable that several of the life events described at the beginning of this chapter may happen for the first time in old age, for example hospitalization for major surgery or accidents, bereavement, changes in social habits and in financial circumstances. In old age these things may be much harder to adapt to. Luker (1979) has pointed out that facilities for adaptation are greatly reduced in old age. At an individual level then, the nurses who understand the potential impact of life events in old age

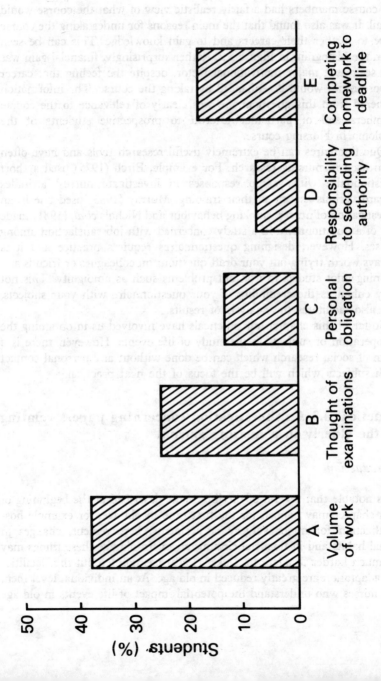

Figure 3.1 Students' first choices concerning sources of anxiety.

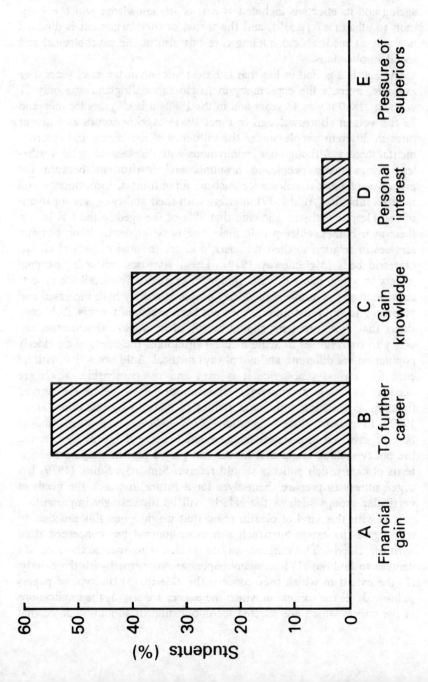

Figure 3.2 Students' first priorities for undertaking Diploma in Nursing course.

may enhance the quality of life for the old people in their care. Barrow-clough & Pinel (1981) state that, 'it is essential that an understanding of ageing and its effects is included as part of the knowledge which is common to all nurses' (p.319), and the thrust of their argument is directed not only at medical and nursing care but also at the psychological and social implications.

Old age is a period in life that is hard to define in terms of years. For example, average life expectancy in Anglo-Saxon England was only 31 years, by 1840 it was 48 years and in the 1980s it is 69 years for men and 75 for women (Barrowclough & Pinel 1981). Ageing occurs at different rates in different people, under the influence of hereditary and environmental factors. Although not synonymous with disease, old age nevertheless brings many people to hospitals and institutions because the processes of normal senescence such as forgetfulness, incontinency and reduced mobility (Auld 1979) interfere with their ability to care for themselves. Despite statistics showing that 90% of the aged in the UK live in their own homes, older people make the heaviest demands on hospital services in relation to their numbers, and are the major users of all but obstetric beds (McGilloway 1979). These statistics reflect a changing society in which many diseases no longer prematurely curtail life expectancy. Instead the numbers of elderly people in society have increased and according to Auld institutions have not been prepared for this. Auld considers that these problems should be solved by nurses. Despite the tendency to train nurses in acute medical situations, the needs of an elderly population are different, and not always medical. Auld notes that with no cure for normal senescence it is care and companionship which are needed, and these are nursing responsibilities if we define the nurses' function as assisting with the activities of daily living (cf. Roper *et al.* 1980). In making these suggestions Auld believes that nurses should become involved in policy making, as she believes it is only by entering the policy-making arena that nurses can play a part in shaping the patterns of care which patients should receive. Similarly, Smith (1979) has urged nurses to prepare themselves for a future in which the needs of particular groups such as the elderly will be increasingly important.

It is with this kind of plea in mind that we designed this practical to investigate the extent to which a nursing journal has concerned itself with the elderly. The simplest way to do this is to analyse the journal's content to find out (1) how many papers are concerned with the elderly; (2) the extent to which they concern the elderly; (3) the type of papers published; (4) the context in which the papers are set; (5) the implications of the papers which are selected for publication. It should be noted that not all the papers submitted to a journal are accepted for publication. They are usually reviewed and on the basis of these reviews the editor makes the final decision whether to include a particular paper or not. You might like to use the technique described above to investigate another aspect of the ageing process.

Method

The aim of our practical was to carry out a content analysis of published material to investigate the extent to which the elderly are represented and in what way. Content analysis is a simple objective technique for measuring the nature of modes of communication, such as papers in journals, television programmes and speeches. For example, a systematic analysis of television advertisements at peak viewing times would enable you to investigate whether there is a tendency to portray families stereotypically, with the mother and daughter cooking and keeping the home pleasant while the father and son engage in outdoor activities. Analysis of recruiting advertisements for nursing in magazines might show a historical trend moving from the portrayal of nurses as female, to portraying them as either male or female.

Compared with interviewing or asking people to complete questionnaires, content analysis has several advantages. You do not need to contact people to take part as the material is usually obtained from written or recorded sources. You are less likely to introduce bias to the results because you are not interacting with your subjects or observing them. It is easy for someone else to replicate your work since the material is usually of a permanent nature, and this means the reliability of your findings can also be checked. On the other hand, the technique can be tedious, require sustained concentration and can take a long time. Sometimes it is necessary to take a sample of your selected material to make it manageable. For example, the *Nursing Times* and *Nursing Mirror* are weekly journals. To compare, say 10 year's issues would mean reading through about a 1000 copies, and this may well not be justified by the purpose of the study. Instead you would chose a representative selection from the possible range, perhaps analysing every tenth issue. The key point is to select a representative sample, as determined by the nature of your study.

The following points should help you organize and complete a content analysis of your own on a topic of particular interest to you.

1. Decide on the topic to be investigated.

2. Decide on the material in which the topic is to be investigated such as nursing journals, television programmes, magazines, etc. The greater the amount of material covered the greater the validity of the findings, but it may be necessary to select representative samples.

3. Decide on the unit for analysis, for example advertisements, documentary programmes, news items, whole journal articles, paragraphs, pictures, etc.

4. Skim rapidly through the material to identify possible categories into which ideas relating to the topic seem to fit. These should be as distinct as possible.

5. Try out the categories on fresh but similar material and modify as necessary. The list of categories should be as comprehensive as possible, but can include a 'miscellaneous' or 'other' section for items not readily incorporated.

6. Draw up data sheets presenting the categories systematically. Use a key to avoid having to write out every category on every data sheet (see, e.g., Tables 3.3, 3.4).

Table 3.3 Key to categories for analysis of units concerned with the elderly for *Journal of Advanced Nursing* 1–7

Type of unit	1a	Empirical study, e.g. survey
	1b	Review, description or discussion paper
	1c	Observation study
	1d	Intervention study
	1e	Editorial
Context of unit	2a	General health care
	2b	Institutional geriatric care
	2c	Medical departments
	2d	Nursing problems
	2e	Miscellaneous
Main implications of unit	3a	Policy, e.g. managerial, educational
	3b	Psychological well-being
	3c	Nursing care
	3d	Research methodology
Rating of degree of concern with elderly	1	Barely mentions elderly
	2	Some mention of the elderly
	3	Mentions the elderly quite a lot
	4	Entirely concerned with the elderly

7. If you want to involve other people in categorizing the material have some practice runs on similar material to ensure that everyone is analysing it in the same way. If others consistently interpret your categories differently you probably need to redefine them.

Sommer & Sommer (1980) have produced more detailed guidelines which you might find useful.

For our investigation we chose to analyse the amount of journal space devoted to papers concerned with the elderly in a nursing journal and the nature of the paper. We chose as our material *Journal of Advanced Nursing*, a British publication with worldwide circulation to which British and overseas authors contribute papers related to a wide range of nursing interests. There are six issues per volume and we decided to look at the seven volumes published since 1976 when the journal began. Our units of analysis consisted of all the papers published in each issue of the journal with the exception of single abstracts, book reviews and news items.

We set about investigating the five areas mentioned in the introduction by skimming through the literature to break them down into categories. The first area concerning the number of papers is simply a matter of counting. For the other four areas we had to produce a more detailed breakdown. The system of content analysis that we designed can be seen in Table 3.3. To measure the extent to which each unit concerned the

Table 3.4 Sample data sheet for *Journal of Advanced Nursing* (1976) **1** (issues I–VI) showing analysis of units concerned with the elderly

| No. of issue | Total units | | Categories | | | |
	Per issue	Concerning elderly	1	2	3	Rating (1–4)
I	9	1	a	a	a	2
II	9	—	—	—	—	—
III	8	—	—	—	—	—
IV	8	1	a	c	b	2
V	10	1	b	d	c	1
		1	b	b	a	3
VI	10	1	c	c	c	1
Totals	54	5	a = 2	a = 1	a = 2	
			b = 2	b = 1	b = 1	
			c = 1	c = 2	c = 2	
			d = 0	d = 1	d = 0	
			e = 0	e = 0		

elderly we produced a rating scale. For the other questions discrete categories had to be designed.

There were a number of problems that arose during the course of our study. It is important to point out that on one or two occasions we found our subgroupings were inadequate and had to be redefined. This meant that we had to analyse the material under the new definitions and indicates both the dynamic nature of the process of content analysis and also its tendency to become tedious! Category 2, relating to the context of the units, was not initially subdivided as the range was so diverse. Instead each unit was briefly described and sorted into groups once all the data had been collected. The use of the rating scale gave us a qualitative guide of the extent to which each paper was concerned with the elderly; rather than just a final total. To some extent the use of this rating scale was subjective. Finally it was not always clear if the units did refer to the elderly. Normally we took the ages 60 years and over as our lowest cut-off point. Sometimes we had to assume that a unit did not include the elderly simply because it did not specify the ages.

Using data sheets as shown in Table 3.4 we analysed each journal, first by counting the number of units in each issue and then the number actually concerned with the elderly. Any unit that seemed to be concerned with the elderly was then analysed according to the categories and rated. We used one data sheet for each volume of six issues.

Results

The results of our analysis fall into four main groups. The first concerns the number of papers concerned with the elderly and the extent to which they are mentioned. Table 3.5 shows that 46 units out of a possible 417 concerned the elderly (approx. 11%). However, if we look at how many of those papers were rated 3 or 4 (particularly concerned with the elderly rather than just mentioning them), the percentage drops to only 5%. The remaining 6% are not specifically concerned with the elderly since they were only rated 1 or 2.

The second set of results relates to the types of units. Table 3.6 shows that there were more empirical and review papers. The papers roughly fall into two groups, those of a research nature (a, c, d) and the rest which are more discursive. To our disappointment there were relatively few papers concerned with interventions.

The third set of results is concerned with the context of the units, which we recorded and then grouped when they were all available. We

Table 3.5 Percentage of units per volume concerned with the elderly and their ratings

Year of vol.	Units per vol.	No. concerned with elderly	% rate	No. of units with each rating 4	3	2	1
1976	54	5	9	—	1	2	2
1977	56	4	7	1	—	—	3
1978	54	3	5.5	1	1	—	1
1979	59	7	12	4	—	—	3
1980	56	6	11	1	1	2	2
1981	68	7	10	5	1	—	1
1982	70	14	20	4	2	1	7
Total	417	46	11	16	6	5	19

For *Journal of Advanced Nursing* 1–7.

found that they fell roughly into the subgroups shown in Table 3.7. From this table we can see that the majority of units concerned with the elderly were related to the contexts of general health care and institutional geriatric care. About half the remainder related to specific medical departments and half to specific nursing problems. Only one was related to research priorities.

Finally we looked at our analysis of the implications of each paper. Table 3.8 shows our findings. We found many more papers were concerned with policy and nursing care than with psychological well-being or research methodology. It was surprising to us to find such a large number of papers concerning policy.

Table 3.6 Analysis by type of units concerned with the elderly

Type of unit	1976	1977	1978	1979	1980	1981	1982	Total
a Empirical study (e.g. survey)	2	1	1	3	2	2	5	16
b Review, description or discussion paper	2	2	1	2	3	3	4	17
c Observation study	1	—	—	—	—	—	1	2
d Intervention study	—	1	1	1	1	2	2	8
e Editorial	—	—	—	1	—	—	2	3
Total	5	4	3	7	6	7	14	46

For *Journal of Advanced Nursing* 1–7.

Table 3.7   Contexts of the units concerned with the elderly

Subgroup	Description	Total
A General health care	Health visiting, preventive health care, non-specific health care, community care	17
B Institutional geriatric care	Psychogeriatrics, geriatrics	16
C Medical departments	Dermatology, intensive care, outpatients, diabetes	6
D Nursing problems	Pressure sores, incontinence, confusion	6
E Miscellaneous	Research priorities	1
		46

For *Journal of Advanced Nursing* **1–7**.

Table 3.8   Implications of the units concerned with the elderly

Implications	Year							Total
	1976	1977	1978	1979	1980	1981	1982	
a Policy	2	1	2	5	3	1	6	20
b Psychological well-being	1	1	0	—	—	1	2	5
c Nursing care	2	2	1	—	3	5	6	19
d Research methodology	—	—	—	2	—	—	—	2
Total	5	4	3	7	6	7	14	46

For *Journal of Advanced Nursing* **1–7**.

Discussion

The results of our content analysis enable us to describe the nature and extent of the journal units which are concerned in some way with the elderly. As few as 5% of the papers included in the seven volumes which we investigated were primarily concerned with the elderly. It may be significant that in 1982 the number of papers pertinent to the topic doubled. 1981 was the International Year of the Disabled and perhaps it drew attention in some way to elderly people, causing a spate of papers. We cannot as yet tell if this increase will continue. It may in the end prove to be an isolated peak.

Approximately half of units mentioning the elderly reported some kind of research. This could be an encouraging indication that a number of people are busy finding things out, although review papers are often the first important step. However, we can only conclude from our analysis that this pattern occurs in this journal. It may not be a true reflection of the actual state of affairs in the nursing world. It is interesting that more of the units were concerned with the contexts of general health care and institutional care, rather than with specific nursing problems, and that several units related to specific medical contexts. There are nurses working in all these areas and it might have been useful to see how often it was nurses writing the units as opposed to doctors or clinical psychologists, for example. Our analysis of the contexts was not at all sensitive to this interesting and important point. Our final set of results concerning the implications of each unit indicated that policy and nursing care were implicated most. This balance is hardly surprising in a journal which is about nursing and is 'advanced'. We have no way of telling the status of its readership from this analysis, but matters of policy and nursing care have been given more weighting. Again this is not necessarily a reflection of nursing, it only describes the content of this journal. If another journal such as *Nursing Research* was analysed the implications might show a different trend.

In the introduction to this chapter we saw that nurses were being encouraged to undertake activities related to policy making for the elderly and to increase their understanding of medical, nursing, sociological and psychological factors in this cause. Only sociological implications have not been mentioned specifically in our analysis of this journal, but it would appear that the needs perceived by a number of authors are being addressed by only 5% of those papers published in *Journal of Advanced Nursing*. This shows how content analysis can be used to investigate a particular issue or problem. As a research tool it is particularly attractive for those lacking the resources to undertake more rigorous field studies. It also produces other topics of interest that are worthy of investigation in their own right. We hope this practical has given you some ideas for you to undertake a content analysis of your own on some issue concerning the elderly and nursing.

Conclusion

In this chapter we have looked briefly at three life events which may be of particular relevance to nurses: becoming a parent, deciding to take a further course of study as a nurse and caring for the elderly. We have not looked at them all from the same point of view and each may matter to you in different ways according to whether you have personal experience of the situation or a professional concern with it. The three areas though enabled us to learn something about life events in relation to human development and in relation to nursing. You may have realized that some life events such as changes in eating habits or financial circumstances can be caused by other life events such as illness or pregnancy so that cause and effect are hard to distinguish from each other. This illustrates the complexity of this field of study, but it also indicates for nurses the value of understanding something of the background from which our patients are drawn. For example, we saw earlier how the meaning that a person attaches to an event can be measured and compared with others. We saw too that stressful events can be linked with illness. We can apply this in our own experience to nursing. A familiar situation might be one from a surgical ward where two people have the same operation but one recovers far more quickly than the other. If we have been able to get to know these patients as individuals, we may realize that the operation is a much more important life event for one than the other. While our nursing experience may give us a rough guide as to how long recovery from a particular operation should take, our knowledge about life events may help us to understand when a patient does not appear to be responding as we would expect, assuming there are no complications such as infection.

Since the knowledge available concerning life events seems to emphasize the perceptions of individuals in relation to the things which happen to them, a patient-orientated, individualized approach to nursing care would seem to be supported. Similarly, the traditional approach in nurse education has been one that emphasizes the physiological and medical aspects of the work. The work of psychologists, however, on matters such as life events, we believe, offers nurses an exciting further dimension to their knowledge about the care of human beings and indicates the importance of nursing patients as individuals. The psychology of life-span development has also been a neglected one in nurse education and we hope this chapter will go some way toward rectifying the balance even though we have only touched on small areas of the subject.

Summary

Three research techniques were described in this chapter: interviewing, questionnaire design and content analysis. All three were used to investigate important aspects of personal development, referred to as life events. We stressed that interviews and questionnaires should be piloted with a few people before being used more extensively but are powerful research tools. Content analysis, on the other hand, was seen to be more limited in its scope but a valuable means of analysing written and spoken material. Finally, the importance to nurses of investigating the psychological aspects of development was emphasized.

References

Auld, M G (1979) Nursing in a changing society. *Journal of Advanced Nursing* **6**, 319–325

Barrowclough, F & Pinel, C (1981) The process of ageing. *Journal of Advanced Nursing* **6**, 319–325

Birch, J (1975) *To Nurse or Not to Nurse* London: Royal College of Nursing

Brown, G W & Harris, T (1978) *Origins of Depression* London: Tavistock

Clark, J M (1981) Communication in nursing. *Nursing Times* **77**, 12–18

Cooper, G L (1982) Psychosocial stress and cancer. *Bulletin of the British Psychological Society* **35**, 456–459

Gunderson, E K E & Rahe, R H (1974) *Life Stress and Illness* Springfield, Illinois: C C Thomas

Hoffman, L & Hoffman, M (1973) The value of children to parents. In J T Fawcett (ed.) *Psychological Perspectives on Population* New York: Basic Books

Hoffman, L W & Manis, J D (1978) Parental satisfaction and dissatisfaction. In R M Lerner & G B Spanier (eds) *Child Influences on Marital and Family Interaction* London: Academic Press

Holmes, T H & Rahe, R H (1967) The Social Readjustment Rating Scale. *Journal of Psychosomatic Research* **11**, 213–218

Lewin, M (1979) *Understanding Psychological Research* New York: John Wiley and Sons

Luker, K (1979) Measuring life satisfaction in an elderly population. *Journal of Advanced Nursing* **4**, 503–511

McGilloway, F A (1979) Care of the elderly: a national and international issue. *Journal of Advanced Nursing* **4**, 545–554

Miller, T W (1981) Life events scaling: clinical methodological issues. *Nursing Research* **30**, 316–320

Moser, C A & Kalton, G (1971) *Survey Methods in Social Investigation* London: Heinemann

Murray, M (1983) Role conflict and intention to leave nursing. *Journal of Advanced Nursing* **8**, 29–31

Nichols, K A, Springford, V & Searle, J (1981) An investigation of distress and discontent in various types of nursing. *Journal of Advanced Nursing* **6**, 311–318

Nicholson, J (1980) *Seven Ages* London: Fontana

Oakley, A (1980) *Women Confined: Towards a Sociology of Childbirth* Oxford: Martin Robertson

Parry, G, Shapiro, D A & Davies, L (1981) Reliability of life-event ratings: an independent replication. *British Journal of Clinical Psychology* **20**, 133–134

Rapoport, R & Rapoport, R N (1977) *Fathers, Mothers and Others* London: Routledge and Kegan Paul

Roper, N, Logan, W & Tierney, A (1980) *The Elements of Nursing* Edinburgh: Churchill Livingstone

Slater, R (1982) Questionnaire design. In G Breakwell, H Foot & R Gilmour (eds) *Social Psychology. A Practical Manual* Leicester/London: The British Psychological Society/ Macmillan Press

Smith, J P (1979) Reality shock for nursing educators (editorial). *Journal of Advanced Nursing* **4**, 235–236

Sommer, R & Sommer, B B (1980) *A Practical Guide to Behavioral Research. Tools and Techniques* New York: Oxford University Press

Steptoe, A (1981) *Psychological Factors in Cardiovascular Disorders* London: Academic Press

CHAPTER 4

PERCEIVING OTHERS

In judging what another person is like, especially a stranger, we often make inferences based on rather superficial cues. Hence, for example, attractive people often get judged more favourably (Argyle & Trower 1979; Nordholm 1980) and it is on the basis of this kind of information that people are stereotyped. A stereotype is a simplified belief that all members of a certain group are alike. For example, all of us are likely to have stereotyped ideas about what consultants or theatre sisters are like. The main danger with stereotyping is that it can lead to prejudice and to discrimination against groups of people. It may, however, also serve to reduce uncertainty to the extent that some initial contact can be made. If all we know about a patient is that he or she is a university professor our view of what professors are like may enable us to initiate conversation and this interaction gives us the opportunity to modify our opinions.

Another way in which we judge other people is on the basis of our own models of personality. It may be that if we are told someone is ambitious we may associate this trait with others, such as ruthlessness and coldness. The set of rules whereby we make inferences of this kind are known as 'implicit personality theories'. Such theories are likely to have in-built biases and perhaps people who could be described as 'professional person perceivers' (including nurses) need these measured and corrected (Cook 1979).

Over the last few years researchers into person perception have become increasingly interested in what people think are the reasons for behaviour. To some extent things happen because of the situations in which people find themselves. Few would blame a patient hospitalized with cancer for the illness, although teenage victims of motor-cycle accidents might be blamed for their resulting injuries. Inferences about the causes of behaviour are investigated under the heading of 'attribution theory' which as Cook (1979) notes 'focuses more particularly on the circumstances and the past events than on the present behaviour, and argues that these are more important in judging someone's behaviour than what is actually perceived, or what actually happens' (p.60).

Clearly the question of how we judge other people is of great importance in nursing. It relates particularly to the kind of professional decisions nurses have to take and to the development of good nurse–patient relations. Cook's (1979) extensive review of research into the psychology of interpersonal perception is an excellent starting point for a more detailed consideration of this field. It may, however, be Cook's conclusion that is of immediate interest. He concludes that people's judgements of others are for the most part very inaccurate. This finding is of crucial significance for professionals who have to rely on their ability to understand others to satisfy their goals. Consequently, the study of how nurses perceive patients is of great concern. The practicals that follow examine some of the techniques which can be used in exploring this question.

Practical 4.1 Perceiving patient characteristics

Introduction

This practical is designed to investigate how we judge other people, especially patients. It appears that we are likely to make judgements on the basis of rather superficial cues such as appearance, and socio-economic factors such as occupation. In the case of patients we are also likely to take the person's medical diagnosis into account. Furthermore, as already discussed in this chapter, we often attribute degrees of blame or responsibility to the patient: that is we are likely to respond differently to a patient who we consider could have avoided becoming unwell or hospitalized.

Stockwell (1972) in her well known study has shown that a number of factors affect how nurses distinguish between popular and unpopular patients. She found that reasons for patients' unpopularity were often related to personality factors as well as physical defects. A certain amount of stereotyping and prejudice were also found. Hence, for example, patients of foreign nationality were more unpopular, as were long-stay patients.

Given the problems involved in judging other people it is important for nurses to have some idea of the kind of influences which affect their own judgements. This is the aim of the following practical.

Method

This practical should be carried out with the whole class as subjects. You will need to be divided into two groups. For our study we used a group of nurses studying for the Diploma in Nursing. The task has two parts. In the first each group assesses certain characteristics of a patient on the basis of a brief description. The patient characteristics to be assessed are shown in Table 4.1 and have been taken to some extent from the work of Stockwell (1972).

In Appendix III there are two portraits of patients who you should imagine have just been hospitalized. (You should not look at these until

Table 4.1 Patient characteristics for Practical 4.1

Consider the patient characteristics listed below and using a 4-point scale rate the extent to which you think each will apply to the person described. For example, if you think that the patient will be very cheerful mark 4, somewhat cheerful mark 3, somewhat unhappy mark 2 or very unhappy mark 1.

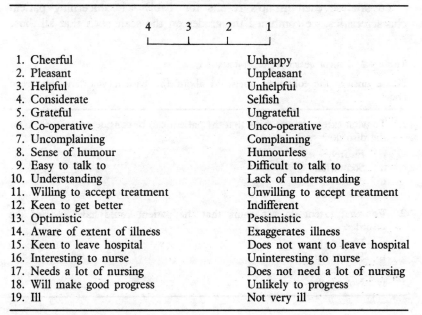

1. Cheerful	Unhappy
2. Pleasant	Unpleasant
3. Helpful	Unhelpful
4. Considerate	Selfish
5. Grateful	Ungrateful
6. Co-operative	Unco-operative
7. Uncomplaining	Complaining
8. Sense of humour	Humourless
9. Easy to talk to	Difficult to talk to
10. Understanding	Lack of understanding
11. Willing to accept treatment	Unwilling to accept treatment
12. Keen to get better	Indifferent
13. Optimistic	Pessimistic
14. Aware of extent of illness	Exaggerates illness
15. Keen to leave hospital	Does not want to leave hospital
16. Interesting to nurse	Uninteresting to nurse
17. Needs a lot of nursing	Does not need a lot of nursing
18. Will make good progress	Unlikely to progress
19. Ill	Not very ill

you have read this Method section.) One group should fill in the scale shown in Table 4.1 for the patient shown on page 141, and the other group should do the same for the patient shown on page 142. You should follow the instructions shown in Table 4.1 and be sure to grade each of the characteristics shown. After you have done this (and before you look at the other description) complete the second part of the practical by answering the questions shown in Table 4.2 about the same patient. Having done both parts of the practical, compare the two descriptions of the patients in Appendix III.

Results

By now you will not only have realized that the descriptions are different but you will be aware that they differ on only one characteristic, that of the diagnosis. In one instance we are assessing a man with cirrhosis of the liver, an illness which can be associated with heavy drinking, making it easy to attribute blame to the patient for having acquired the disease. In the other case the disorder is more neutral, a simple hernia repair. This enables us to compare how our perceptions of a patient's characteristics might be affected simply by the reason for the person being hospitalized.

To analyse each group's results for Table 4.1 concerning patient characteristics, we combined the grades on the scale such that all those

---

Table 4.2   Patient questions for Practical 4.1

Please answer the following questions about the patient you have just read about

---

1.   To what extent do you think that the patient can be considered *responsible* for the disorder?

   i   Entirely
   ii Somewhat
   iii A little
   iv Not at all

2.   To what extent do you think that the patient could have *avoided* the disorder?

   i   Entirely
   ii Somewhat
   iii A little
   iv Not at all

within each group who marked 4 or 3 for a particular characteristic were counted together, as were those who marked either 2 or 1. Our results are presented in Table 4.3. Thus for the characteristics uncomplaining–complaining the patient with cirrhosis of the liver, was scored 4 or 3 by ten nurses and 2 or 1 by two nurses. The same characteristic for the hernia patient were awarded a 4 or 3 by six nurses and a 2 or 1 by three nurses. This combining of the scores makes it easy to make comparisons when the data from both groups are assembled together.

Our results enable us to draw some tentative conclusions concerning how nurses might perceive two different types of patient. For example, it is thought that the patient suffering from cirrhosis of the liver will be less cheerful, more unhelpful, more ungrateful, slightly more unco-operative, more difficult to talk to, more willing to accept treatment and less likely

Table 4.3 Comparison of nurses' rating of patient characteristics associated with diagnosis

Patient characteristics	Cirrhosis		Hernia	
	4 & 3	2 & 1	4 & 3	2 & 1
Cheerful–unhappy	7	5	8	1
Pleasant–unpleasant	10	2	8	1
Helpful–unhelpful	8	4	8	1
Considerate–selfish	7	5	6	3
Grateful–ungrateful	5	7	7	2
Co-operative–unco-operative	8	4	8	1
Uncomplaining–complaining	10	2	6	3
Sense of humour–humourless	7	5	7	2
Easy to talk to–difficult to talk to	6	6	7	2
Understanding–lack of understanding	7	5	6	3
Willing to accept treatment–unwilling	10	2	5	4
Keen to get better–indifferent	9	3	9	0
Optimistic–pessimistic	7	5	7	2
Aware of extent of illness–exaggerates illness	10	2	5	4
Keen to leave hospital–does not want to leave	12	0	9	0
Interesting to nurse–uninteresting to nurse	8	4	6	3
Needs a lot of nursing–does not need a lot of nursing	8	4	1	8
Will make good progress–unlikely to progress	3	9	9	0
Ill–not very ill	11	1	2	7

to exaggerate the extent of the illness than the same patient would be if suffering from a hernia. Both are considered equally keen to leave hospital, but while the hernia patient is considered to have an excellent prognosis the cirrhosis patient is not. These tentative conclusions are based on a simple comparison of scores for each group. The group sizes in our experiment are uneven ($n = 12$ and 9) therefore one must check that differences really do exist. For example, the question of how interesting nursing each person is drew scores of 8, 4 and 6, 3. These ratio scores are identical indicating that there is no difference in how interesting they are to nurse.

Wherever the actual ratio of the numbers to each other is different, there is a difference in perception of the patient characteristic. The greater the difference between the scores in each group, the greater the difference in perception. An example of a characteristic showing a great difference would be willingness to accept treatment. This scores 10, 2 (cirrhosis patient) against 5, 4 (hernia patient). Thus while those scoring the hernia patient differed very slightly in their opinion (he is regarded as almost equally likely to accept or reject treatment) the opinion of the second group is much stronger; the cirrhosis patient is considered much more willing to accept treatment than not to accept treatment. Our results also show that the patient with cirrhosis of the liver is considered by the nurses to need a lot of nursing and to be very ill, opinions which reflect not so much patient behaviour as perceived need for forms of nursing care.

We then analysed the responses to the set questions we asked in Table 4.2. Again we combined the categories to simplify the data ('entirely' with 'somewhat' and 'a little' with 'not at all'). Our results are shown in Table 4.4. We can see very clearly from these that it was felt by our nurses that the patient suffering from cirrhosis of the liver was held to be more responsible for his disorder and better able to have avoided it than the person suffering from a hernia.

Table 4.4 Attribution of responsibility to patients by nurses for each condition

Question [a]	Cirrhosis		Hernia	
	Patient blamed	Patient not blamed	Patient blamed	Patient not blamed
1	10	2	2	7
2	10	2	3	6

[a] Questions as given in Table 4.2.

Discussion

This practical experiment demonstrated clearly that nurses are capable of judging patients differently according to the medical diagnosis assigned to them. These differences related both to aspects of nursing care and to broad characteristics of patient behaviour. From the results of Stockwell's (1972) study and a review by Najman *et al.* (1982) which indicated that 'abusers' (of drugs, alcohol, etc.) are less popular, we would expect that if our patient were suffering from cirrhosis of the liver it is likely he would be seen as more unpopular than if suffering from a hernia. Such a finding has important implications for nursing.

The second part of this practical experiment investigated attribution of responsibility. Earlier in this chapter we discussed how people often try to attribute causes to another person's behaviour. We found in this practical that the patient with cirrhosis of the liver was heavily blamed for his disorder. It was felt that he was responsible and that he could have avoided becoming ill. In this sense it can be said that the patient was the cause of his own illness. In contrast, the patient suffering from a hernia appeared less likely to be blamed for his illness.

In analysing your results you may find that your findings are similar to ours. However, if they differ, what could be the reasons for this? Our subjects were experienced nurses. Perhaps experience plays a role in anticipating patient characteristics for different diagnoses. If you tried the experiment with very junior nurses who perhaps did not know what cirrhosis of the liver can imply about drinking habits, would you expect a different set of results? You can run the experiment using types of diagnoses other than the ones we have suggested. Another variation would be to write two new identical descriptions of a patient with the same diagnosis but make one male and one female and see what results this brings.

It must of course be noted that this practical is somewhat unrealistic and does not have the 'ecological validity' of Stockwell's study. By this we simply mean that Stockwell carried out her research on the wards with practising nurses and actual patients. However, despite this limitation our results are very similar to those of Stockwell and could certainly be predicted from her study. Furthermore they do demonstrate that even as professionals we too have certain biases in the way we view and judge people. Many of us are well aware of speculation about how a small minority of casualty nurses view patients who have attempted suicide (Ryland & King 1982) and this study demonstrates that such a belief is not without foundation. Clearly it does point to the need for nurses to be aware of their own biases in predicting behaviour and for them to counteract this when working with certain types of patients.

Practical 4.2 Ward characteristics: a study in person perception

Introduction

As we have shown in Practical 4.1 the way we judge unfamiliar people is clearly influenced by various details that we know about them. Our patient with cirrhosis of the liver was seen in a less favourable light than if the same person had been suffering from a hernia. It is likely that this process of categorizing patients will affect the extent to which nurses enjoy working on some wards rather than others. Furthermore it is probable that the ways in which nurses view their own career aspirations and interests will also affect how much they enjoy nursing different types of patients.

The aim of this practical is to investigate the reasons why nurses prefer nursing patients on some wards rather than others. First, we will investigate your preferences for one ward rather than another so you can compare your choices with those of your colleagues. Secondly, we will get you to give reasons for your choices to see what factors seem to be the most significant in determining them.

Method

This practical is best carried out as a group exercise. It is divided into two parts as shown below. Try not to discuss your responses with your colleagues until all the class has completed the practical. In selecting the wards for this practical we deliberately restricted the choice to allow a great diversity of reasons to be elicited. We carried out the study with our group of nurses who were studying for the Diploma in Nursing.

Part 1. Rank order the following list according to the extent to which you would most like to nurse patients on these wards. Rank 1 should be the ward you would most prefer to work on.

Psychiatric	1	_____
Geriatric	2	_____
General surgery	3	_____
General medicine	4	_____
Paediatric	5	_____

Part 2. Now give reasons for your first choice, i.e., your most popular ward from the list and for your last choice, i.e., your most unpopular.

Finally write down any other reasons you took into account in rank ordering the wards, according to popularity.

Results

The first stage in analysing the data is to organize the information as shown in Table 4.5. From this Table it can be seen that five of the group members ranked psychiatric nursing as the most popular, whereas eight ranked it as the least popular. This suggests some division of opinion concerning psychiatric nursing. Although nobody ranked geriatric nursing as the most popular, the choices were fairly evenly distributed between ranks 2, 3, 4 and 5. More people ranked general surgery as the most popular although it also attracted a few more lower rankings than did general medicine. Paediatric nursing seemed to be ranked more toward the middle, although the ranks allocated were well distributed.

We then produced a rank-order list of preferences for the whole group combined. This was done by summing the ranks total for each ward. For example, the rank total for psychiatric nursing was 70 made up of $(5 \times 1) + (2 \times 2) + (3 \times 3) + (3 \times 4) + (8 \times 5)$. The final rank order and totals are shown in Table 4.6. As can be seen from this general medicine was ranked the most popular despite the fact that eight out of 21 nurses ranked general surgery first as compared with five who ranked general medicine first. This result was brought about by the large number of nurses ranking general medicine second. Despite the number of nurses ranking psychiatric nursing first it was seen to be only marginally more popular than geriatric nursing.

In analysing the second part of this practical we used a similar form of

Table 4.5 Nurses' responses to rank ordering their ward preferences (1 most popular, 5 least popular)

Wards	Ranks				
	1	2	3	4	5
Psychiatric	5	2	3	3	8
Geriatric	0	6	4	6	5
General surgery	8	2	3	6	2
General medicine	5	8	4	3	1
Paediatric	3	3	7	3	5

Table 4.6 Final popularity rankings for selected wards

Rank	Ward	Total rank scores
1st	General medicine	50
2nd	General surgery	55
3rd	Paediatric	67
4th	Psychiatric	70
5th	Geriatric	73

content analysis to that undertaken in Practical 3.3. However, in this instance we were not concerned with quantifying the data but simply grouping the material into appropriate categories. In her study Stockwell (1972) found four categories of reasons, written by nurses for enjoying or not enjoying looking after patients: personality factors, communication factors, attitude factors and nursing factors.

We were able to group our findings into four categories as shown in Table 4.7: career factors, nursing factors, patient characteristics and ward characteristics. We found it possible to group all the reasons given for either liking or disliking nursing patients on specific wards under these four headings. From our data it appeared that equal weighting was given to all four categories, although possibly ward characteristics were mentioned less frequently.

Discussion

From our results we found that nurses do have general reasons for preferring nursing patients on one ward rather than another. Many nurses seem to be influenced by patient characteristics such as the prognosis and the type of disorder. Hence, in our study we found a general dislike of

Table 4.7 Categories of reasons for ranking wards in popularity

Categories	Types of reasons
Nursing career	Past experience; future aspirations; opportunity for study
Nursing activity	Nursing skills required; patients' needs; degree involvement with patients
Patient characteristics	Age; disorder; length of stay; prognosis
Ward characteristics	Staff relations; ward atmosphere

nursing geriatric and psychiatric patients. Stockwell (1972) found that unpopular patients often had associated psychiatric disorders or difficulties in communication and more recently Wilkinson (1982) has found that general-nursing students tend to 'distrust' psychiatric patients.

Our results also suggest that general medicine is an area which does not produce marked negative feelings. Most of our nurses seemed to feel that they could work there even if it were not their first choice. This was not the case with paediatric nursing where it was usually a stated dislike of children which made such nursing unpopular to some of our nurses. General surgery although relatively popular was seen by some to be monotonous and as having too rapid a turnover.

This practical suggests that we make broad generalizations about different areas of nursing in a similar way to the judgements we make concerning individual patients. As Cook (1979) shows us in his book, we tend to select relatively distinctive cues and rely on them to make quite broad generalizations. Hence given the diagnosis of one patient we might infer a number of characteristics we expect to find in that patient. Similarly, given one ward we do have a number of reasons which we can readily bring to mind, concerning why we do or do not like nursing the types of patients we would expect to find there. In both instances we are a little guilty perhaps of making stereotyped responses based on too little evidence.

There are a number of variations you might like to try with this practical. You could see whether or not your own group produces a similar ranking order and by adding different wards you could collect still more detailed information. In eliciting the reasons for ranking different wards you could investigate whether or not you arrive at the same categories as we have. It may be interesting to relate this information to the current or past nursing experiences of the group. Finally, you might like to use the reasons you have collected to produce a more formal measure of ward preferences, possibly in the form of a rating scale. These techniques are discussed in the practical which follows.

Practical 4.3 The use of rating scales in studying person perception

Introduction

Another way of finding out people's feelings or attitudes toward certain issues is to develop a rating scale. The main aim of a rating scale is to provide objective data which can be analysed easily. This is achieved by simplifying the ways in which subjects give you information. Content analysis as shown in Practicals 3.3 and 4.2 is often a good way to collect some ideas about the kind of questions to include on a rating scale. The difficulty with content analysis is that it is not always obvious how to classify the responses. Rating scales are usually designed with this in mind and an attempt is made to ask questions about all the important areas to be covered.

The aim of this practical is for you to design a rating scale about any aspect of nursing which is of interest. To assist you in this exercise the kind of techniques available will be explained and you will be invited to complete a rating scale yourself. The results we collected using rating scales will be reported and discussed to enable you to understand the strengths and limitations of this approach.

Method

There are a variety of techniques that can be used in the design of a rating scale. The most common will be discussed.

1.   Graphic rating scales require that subjects place a mark along a continuous line to express their feelings. An example from a rating scale designed to measure coronary-prone behaviour (Bortner 1969) is shown below.

✓

| Not competitive | Competitive |

The score is obtained by measuring the distance of the tick from the left-hand side of the scale.

2.   A simpler technique that is easier to score is to offer a statement followed by a set number of response categories. For example, a 5-point scale might be: Strongly Agree, Agree, Uncertain, Disagree, Strongly Disagree. It is sometimes helpful to use a 4-point scale which forces the respondent to make a decision. This was one technique used by Stockwell (1972) in her study of the unpopular patient.

3.   The use of a numerical rating scale is similar and provides distinct points for respondents to mark, as shown opposite.

1	2	3	4	5
Entirely true				Entirely false

Often techniques 2 and 3 are combined.

4. Another technique is to ask respondents to mark 'Yes' or 'No' as in Eysenck's Inventory shown in Chapter 2, or to give three choices, 'Yes' '?' 'No'. The former technique forces respondents to make a choice.

5. Respondents can also be given two or more statements from which they are asked to select the one with which they most agree by ticking it. People might be asked, for example, which of the following do they most agree with:

    'Charge nurses/sisters have little influence on hospital policy'
    or 'Charge nurses/sisters have a great deal of influence on hospital policies'.

6. With children a pictorial scale can be used, the most common being 'Smiley Faces' as shown below.

The use of rating scales is very popular as a research tool but similar problems arise as when designing questionnaires especially concerning the wording of questions. Before designing a rating scale the reader should refer to Practical 3.2 on questionnaire design.

In designing a rating scale you should consider the variety of techniques explained above. You should also make sure that the questions are clear and that your respondents (probably your colleagues) understand how to complete the scale. Do make sure that you cover all the important areas about the topic you plan to investigate. It might be sensible to ask a few informal questions first in the same way we did in our use of content analysis in Practical 4.2. Hence, if you are interested in investigating the attitudes of nurses toward the care of the terminally ill, a starting point is simply to ask colleagues an open question such as 'What are your feelings about caring for the terminally ill?'. From the information gained by this technique you will find it easier to select topics on which you want to ask more specific questions. Once you have designed the scale you should

Table 4.8 Scale for measuring attitudes toward mildly and severely mentally retarded persons

Please circle the one response which best expresses your agreement or disagreement with each of the items shown for both mildly and severely retarded children.

1. Special classes are justified for mildly/severely retarded children
2. Normal children also benefit when mildly/severely retarded children are integrated into regular classes
3. Integrating mildly/severely retarded children into regular classes contributes to negative behaviour patterns on the part of the 'normal' children
4. Mildly/severely retarded children should go to special schools where 'normal' children do not attend
5. Mildly/severely retarded children would learn more if they were integrated into regular classes
6. The prescence of a mildly/severely retarded child in a regular class impedes the educational progress of the child's 'normal' peers
7. Mildly/severely retarded children may reach their potential but will never be able to function on the level of their 'normal' age or grade peers
8. Mildly/severely retarded children should not be placed in institutions
9. Integration of the mildly/severely retarded child into regular classes will improve the child's acceptance by his or her 'normal' peers
10. The mildly/severely retarded child will feel inadequate in the regular classroom
11. Mildly/severely retarded children have a right to public education
12. The transfer of mildly/severely retarded children to regular classes creates no major problems other than the need for resource teachers
13. Mildly/severely retarded children are more likely to be discipline problems in regular classes than in special classes
14. Mildly/severely retarded children can learn to live normal lives

Siperstein, G N (1979) A scale for measuring (parents'/teachers')attitudes toward mildly and severely mentally retarded persons. Unpublished manuscript, University of Massachusetts, Boston. Reprinted with kind permission of the author.

collect together a number of responses and analyse the results as appropriate.

However, before you design your scale you might find it helpful to complete and score a rating scale which has already been tested. This scale designed by G. N. Siperstein (unpublished work) measures the attitudes of parents and teachers toward mildly and severely mentally retarded children and focuses on the topic of integration into school and community settings. Not surprisingly it had been found in an earlier study that teachers and parents felt that integration was more appropriate

Key:	Strongly Agree	Agree	Uncertain	Disagree	Strongly Disagree					
	SA	A	U	D	SD					

	Mildly retarded					Severely retarded				
1.	SA	A	U	D	SD	SA	A	U	D	SD
2.	SA	A	U	D	SD	SA	A	U	D	SD
3.	SA	A	U	D	SD	SA	A	U	D	SD
4.	SA	A	U	D	SD	SA	A	U	D	SD
5.	SA	A	U	D	SD	SA	A	U	D	SD
6.	SA	A	U	D	SD	SA	A	U	D	SD
7.	SA	A	U	D	SD	SA	A	U	D	SD
8.	SA	A	U	D	SD	SA	A	U	D	SD
9.	SA	A	U	D	SD	SA	A	U	D	SD
10.	SA	A	U	D	SD	SA	A	U	D	SD
11.	SA	A	U	D	SD	SA	A	U	D	SD
12.	SA	A	U	D	SD	SA	A	U	D	SD
13.	SA	A	U	D	SD	SA	A	U	D	SD
14.	SA	A	U	D	SD	SA	A	U	D	SD

for the mildly rather than severely retarded children (Siperstein & Gottlieb 1978).

The rating scale is shown in Table 4.8 and you should answer each question for both the mildly and severely mentally retarded. This will give you a measure of your feelings concerning integration for both groups. From these data it is possible to look at three separate issues: the differences if any between the two groups; profiles of how each group is perceived; an overall score on a scale from extremely negative to extremely positive.

Our results for our diploma in nursing students are presented below. You might like to collect the results of your colleagues together and compare them with our findings before carrying out the second part of this study, the design of a rating scale of your own.

Table 4.9 Number of nurses selecting each response category for mildly and severely retarded people

Question	Mildly retarded			Severely retarded		
	Agree	Uncertain	Disagree	Agree	Uncertain	Disagree
1	17	3	0	19	0	1
2	13	2	5	3	5	12
3	0	6	14	8	7	5
4	1	5	14	9	3	8
5	12	3	5	2	4	14
6	5	6	9	13	2	6
7	10	1	9	19	1	0
8	18	0	2	9	4	7
9	18	2	0	8	5	7
10	9	7	4	10	4	6
11	19	1	0	15	2	3
12	10	4	6	0	2	18
13	3	5	12	9	5	6
14	17	1	2	1	4	15

Results

The results we collected are shown in Table 4.9. As you can see we have combined the categories 'Strongly Agree' with 'Agree' and 'Strongly Disagree' with 'Disagree'. Our results are similar to those of Siperstein & Gottlieb and show that our nurses had different views regarding the integration of mildly retarded children as compared with the severely retarded. For example, question 2 clearly discriminates between the two groups, and suggests that our nurses feel that normal children could only benefit from integration with the mildly retarded not the severely retarded.

From Siperstein's scale it is also possible to calculate an overall score concerning whether positive or negative attitudes are held toward the two different groups. This will involve you in converting the responses you have just made into numbers. On each question a score ranging from 1 to 5 is given, 1 representing the most negative response and 5 the most positive. For the negatively worded questions (1, 3, 4, 6, 7, 10 and 13), respondents score from 1 for 'Strongly Agree' to 5 for 'Strongly Disagree'. For the remaining items respondents score from 5 for 'Strongly Agree' to 1 for 'Strongly Disagree'. Final scores range from 14 (extremely negative) to 70 (extremely positive), that is from a mean score of 1 to a mean score of 5.

We calculated each individual's score, added them all together, then divided by the number of subjects to get the mean scores for our sample. The mean score for attitudes toward mildly retarded children was 3.5 (slightly positive) and towards severely retarded children 2.6 (slightly negative). This shows a clear difference.

Discussion

As one would expect our data confirm the general finding that mildly retarded children are perceived differently from severely retarded children. This predictable finding shows that the scale we used does in fact discriminate and to that extent it is useful. Your rating scale may only measure attitudes toward a single group of people or one specific topic. If this is the case you might find it interesting to collect information from two different groups of people, say nurses and the laypeople with less relevant knowledge. This would allow you to make a comparison with your scale.

From our data it is also possible to build up a profile of how our nurses view the two different groups. It was generally believed that normal children would benefit more when mildly rather than severely retarded children were integrated into regular classes and that the severely retarded would be more likely to contribute to negative behaviour patterns on the part of normal children. It was also felt that mildly retarded children would be more suited to special schools, that compared with severely retarded children they would learn more and that they were less likely to impede the educational progress of normal children. Similarly, it was felt that the severely retarded would never fully function normally and that mildly retarded children should not be placed in institutions. There was a strong feeling that integration of mildly retarded children would improve their acceptance by their peers but that integration of the severely retarded would create problems. It was also clear that the mildly retarded were more likely to be able to lead normal lives. You should be able to build up similar profiles using your scale even though it might only apply to one group of people or set of events.

The final score we derived was a total relating to the degree of negative and positive feelings felt. As expected attitudes toward mildly retarded children were more favourable. If your scale is organized in the same way you might be able to produce a total for your scale. The advantage of doing this is that it makes overall comparisons quite easy. A disadvantage is that the design of the scale might be restricted in some way to produce a single score.

The use of rating scales is a very structured way of collecting information about the way patients are seen. It enables a series of questions to be asked that gives a more comprehensive view than that obtained from the first practical in this chapter. In that practical the scale used was imposed without any prior research into whether it was appropriate. It is important in designing rating scales to undertake some kind of pilot study, as suggested earlier, to produce a scale which measures what you want it to measure.

Conclusion

From these three practicals it can be seen that it is possible to investigate the attitudes people hold about others. The first practical showed that experienced nurses perceived people with different diagnoses in different ways. These nurses' attitudes toward two patients varied with regard to beliefs about how each patient would behave, what their personalities would be like, what it would be like to nurse them and whether they thought the patients could be blamed for their illness. We were not able to investigate whether these differences in perception would affect how the nurses might look after these patients. However, it is interesting to note that Stockwell (1972) did find that less popular patients were treated differently from the more popular ones in that the nurses tended to interact more negatively with the less popular patients.

We began the chapter, by reporting Cook's (1979) proposal that 'professional person perceivers' such as nurses may need to have their 'implicit personality theories' measured and corrected. One step toward understanding our attitudes as nurses might be to read more widely. Miller's (1979) discussion paper, which directly concerns nursing, gives several suggestions as to why and how unhelpful attitudes may develop. This is a good starting point. We cannot say from our practical whether the development of different attitudes toward some patients is inevitable, or even if it is unhelpful, but the practical does serve to illustrate one objective way of finding out more about nurses' attitudes.

The second practical looked briefly at nurse's preferences for different types of nursing and found that the reasons for preferring different types of wards were related to four main factors. Three of these concerned aspects of the work (patient characteristics, ward characteristics and nursing activities) and one concerned personal experience. With regard to the three work-related reasons, discussions with our students indicated strong preferences for working in particular types of wards. They expressed quite definite likes and dislikes, for example regarding patient turnover rates, ages of patients, how much one was able to spend time with patients and whether there was likely to be a high death rate. With regard to personal experience, there was a tendency for nurses to feel more negative toward types of wards in which they had no experience. This suggests that the current training pattern for nurses in which experience is gained in a number of special areas such as psychiatry or geriatrics may serve an important purpose in minimizing negative discrimination. We will be looking further at factors relating to the work situation in Chapter 7.

Miller (1979) has pointed out that attitudes cannot be directly observed, but must be inferred either from an individual's self-report or from behaviour. In the third practical we provided a tested self-report measure about nurses' attitudes toward two degrees of mentally handicapped people. We did this in two ways, by presenting lists of statements and asking subjects to rank their degree of agreement with them and, secondly, by comparing the same ratings according to how much they reflected a positive or negative attitude toward the two groups of mentally handicapped people. Our findings enabled us to build up a profile or description of the nurses' attitudes and to compare these with findings from other groups such as parents or teachers. Not surprisingly we found close similarities between all groups.

These three practicals all raise the same fundamental problem. From the data we have collected it is not possible to know whether our nurses behave in a manner which is consistent with their attitudes. This is an issue which confronts all researchers using pencil and paper measures of behaviour. It is also the case of course that our attitudes are always susceptible to change. What we experience is likely to affect how we feel and there is a strong case for giving people a wide range of experience to help modify their attitudes. This argument is even more important for those professions involved in caring for others in a wide variety of situations. We hope that this chapter has taken you a step further in analysing and understanding your own attitudes.

Summary

In this chapter we emphasized the topic of attitudes and designed three practicals to demonstrate some techniques for investigating them. These practicals involved rating scales, but also included material of a less restricted kind in which students were invited to express their own feelings. We have concentrated on how we judge others but we have not taken into account how these people might be judging us or affecting our reactions to them. Although we have investigated attitudes in our practicals, we have not looked at how they actually affect behaviour between people. This topic is the subject of the next chapter.

References

Argyle, M & Trower, P (1979) *Person to Person. Ways of Communicating* London: Harper and Row

Bortner, R W (1969) A short rating scale as a potential measure of pattern 'A' behavior. *Journal of Chronic Diseases* **22**, 87–91

Cook, M (1979) *Perceiving Others. The Psychology of Interpersonal Perception* London: Methuen

Miller, A E (1979) Nurses' attitudes towards their patients. *Nursing Times* **75**, 1929–1933

Najman, J M, Klein, D & Munro, C (1982) Patient characteristics negatively stereotyped by doctors. *Social Science and Medicine* **16**, 1781–1789

Nordholm, L A (1980) Beautiful patients are good patients. *Social Science and Medicine* **14A**, 81–84

Ryland, R & King, M (1982) An overdose of attitudes. *Nursing Mirror* **154**, 40–41

Siperstein, G N & Gottlieb, J (1978) Parents' and teachers' attitudes toward mildly and severely retarded children. *Mental Retardation* **16**, 321–322

Stockwell, F (1972) *The Unpopular Patient* London: Royal College of Nursing

Wilkinson, D (1982) The effects of brief psychiatric training on the attitudes of general nursing students to psychiatric patients. *Journal of Advanced Nursing* **7**, 239–254

CHAPTER 5

INTERPERSONAL UNDERSTANDING

In the previous chapter we investigated some of the factors which influence our judgements of other people. One of the most important reasons for undertaking this kind of research is that the way we behave toward others affects the way they in turn respond to us. If you believe that a patient is confused, you will behave in a certain way toward that person. The nature of your initial communication will determine the range of responses available to the patient, who, if not confused, might react aggressively or show frustration. This in turn affects the way the conversation continues. The processes involved in interpersonal communication have been analysed as a set of social skills which can be developed through training (cf. Trower *et al.* 1978; Hargie *et al.* 1981). Consequently, it should be possible to improve our ability to initiate and maintain effective communication.

In communicating a verbal message, we rely on the spoken language we use and the non-verbal cues which accompany it. Both these channels of communication are important. In the following chapter we review some research which has examined the content of verbal messages and the effect of organization on memory. However, it is equally important to point out that how we speak will also affect the kind of responses we elicit from others. This topic has been extensively researched into by Giles and his colleagues (cf. Giles & Powesland 1975). It has been shown that the way we speak, especially concerning volume, tone, clarity and speed, suggests to others the kind of people we are. The research has shown, for example, that personality, social class and professional status are just a few characteristics which are inferred from the way we speak. Whether such inferences are accurate is not important; by themselves they affect the ways in which others respond to us and the nature of our communication with them.

Non-verbal cues are also extremely important. The influence of these on social interaction is described by Argyle (1975). Non-verbal cues include facial expression, posture, gaze, how near individuals stand to each other and numerous other facets of behaviour. Perhaps the most important point is that sometimes the non-verbal message is not always the same as that given verbally. For example, a nurse might well be speaking to a patient while at the same time keeping an eye out for the arrival of the consultant. The message the patient will receive is that, although the nurse is talking to me, he or she is more concerned about the arrival of somebody else. This kind of incongruence, which is often referred to as 'leakage' conveys very important information to the recipient of any message and is a crucial factor in any interpersonal communication.

Social skills in the nursing context are the subject of an outstanding review by Davis (1981). He suggests that nurses do have stereotyped perceptions of patients and interact with them accordingly. It also appears from the studies reviewed that nurses find difficulty in initiating, developing and maintaining conversation with their patients. However, as Davis stresses, the social structure of practical nursing is far from conducive to relaxed and effective communication. There is then an agreed need to improve communication in nursing and to help nurses acquire the necessary social skills to become effective communicators. Included in these skills are the qualities and abilities required to have more influence over the work environment and to break down any barriers to communication.

This chapter explores some aspects of interpersonal communication. The first practical is concerned with the degree to which nurses have empathy with the needs of their patients. This involves a simple investigative technique. The next practical is about observation and follows on from the practical in Chapter 1. Although the technique to be used is objective, it is hoped that those participating will learn something about the way they themselves communicate. The final practical is far less structured and involves role playing and similar techniques. It is entirely experiential and illustrates the use of such techniques in psychology. It is hoped that, taken together, these practicals will make you think more carefully and critically about the processes involved in communication.

Practical 5.1   Nurses' predictions of patients' ratings of psychosocial stress

Introduction

This practical is designed to investigate how nurses think patients rate the severity of stressful psychosocial events concerning hospitalization. The ability to put oneself in the place of another is usually referred to as empathy. Nurses in their role of caring for people might be expected to develop empathy for their patients if they are to communicate with them effectively. However, a study by Johnston (1982) has shown that other patients appear to know more about surgical patients' worries than the nurses responsible for them. She suggests that these results show that nurses are not in fact particularly good at identifying the worries of an individual patient.

We thought that this finding might be interesting to investigate from a slightly different perspective. An American study by Volicer & Bohannon (1975) has produced a hospital stress rating scale of particular relevance to medical and surgical patients. They got 261 patients to rank order 49 events related to the experience of hospitalization from the most to the least stressful. The results of this are shown in Table 5.1. The least stressful experience is ranked 1 and the most stressful is ranked 49. We thought that, to investigate how empathic nurses are, we could get them to rank order these events as they thought patients might. This practical describes one way of doing this.

Method

There are two slight difficulties in carrying out this practical. First, the number of psychosocial events identified by Volicer & Bohannon is rather large and hence time-consuming to work with. Secondly, although you can carry this practical out on yourselves, you will be biased by the results obtained from the American study. You can overcome this to some extent by selecting say only 20 events as we did, writing them on cards without their ranks and then carry out the practical say a week later without referring back to Table 5.1. However, it would be better if you could use colleagues with no prior knowledge of the findings as subjects.

Having chosen the events you want to use, randomize them and present them to your subjects on a printed sheet or an overhead projector.

Table 5.1   Assigned rank order for events related to the experience of hospitalization

Assigned rank	Event
1.	Having strangers sleep in the same room with you
2.	Having to eat at different times than you usually do
3.	Having to sleep in a strange bed
4.	Having to wear a hospital gown
5.	Having strange machines around
6.	Being awakened in the night by the nurse
7.	Having to be assisted with bathing
8.	Not being able to get newspapers, radio or TV when you want them
9.	Having a room-mate who has too many visitors
10.	Having to stay in bed or the same room all day
11.	Being aware of unusual smells around you
12.	Having a room-mate who is seriously ill or cannot talk with you
13.	Having to be assisted with a bedpan
14.	Having a room-mate who is unfriendly
15.	Not having friends visit you
16.	Being in a room that is too cold or too hot
17.	Thinking your appearance might be changed after your hospitalization
18.	Being in the hospital during holidays or special family occasions
19.	Thinking you might have pain because of surgery or test procedures
20.	Worrying about your spouse being away from you
21.	Having to eat cold or tasteless food
22.	Not being able to call family or friends on the phone
23.	Being cared for by an unfamiliar doctor
24.	Being put in the hospital because of an accident
25.	Not knowing when to expect things will be done to you
26.	Having the staff be in too much of a hurry
27.	Thinking about losing income because of your illness
28.	Having medications cause you discomfort
29.	Having nurses or doctors talk too fast or use words you can't understand
30.	Feeling you are getting dependent on medications
31.	Not having family visit you
32.	Knowing you have to have an operation
33.	Being hospitalized far away from home
34.	Having a sudden hospitalization you weren't planning to have
35.	Not having your call light answered
36.	Not having enough insurance to pay for your hospitalization
37.	Not having your questions answered by the staff
38.	Missing your spouse
39.	Being fed through tubes
40.	Not getting relief from pain medications
41.	Not knowing the results or reasons for your treatments
42.	Not getting pain medication when you need it
43.	Not knowing for sure what illness you have
44.	Not being told what your diagnosis is

45. Thinking you might lose your hearing
46. Knowing you have a serious illness
47. Thinking you might lose a kidney or some other organ
48. Thinking you might have cancer
49. Thinking you might lose your sight

Volicer, B J & Bohannon, M W (1975) A hospital stress rating scale. *Nursing Research* **24**, 352–359. Copyright by the American Journal of Nursing Company. Reprinted with kind permission of the authors and publishers.

You can dictate them but it takes longer. You can present any number of events from the scale but since we chose 20, the subjects were instructed to rank order the events from 1 to 20, with 1 being the event they thought patients would rank the least stressful and with 20 being the event they thought patients would rank the most stressful. It should be emphasized that they are completing this task not as if they were patients but as they would predict a set of patients might.

We presented a group of 19 diploma in nursing students with the selected events. From the data shown in Table 5.1 we were able to produce an adjusted rank order as shown in Table 5.2, such that the first event mentioned as least stressful was ranked 1, the second was marked 2 and so forth. Hence we had a rank order with which to compare the results from our group of nurses. It might be necessary to set a time limit on this task, say 30 minutes, and not to encourage your subjects to have tied ranks.

Results

To produce an overall rank order for our nurses we simply summed the total ranks awarded to each event by each student to produce 20 totals. These totals were then used to rank the data as shown in Table 5.2 in the final column. Hence it can be seen from this Table that 'Having strangers sleep in same room with you' was ranked first in the Volicer & Bohannon study and third by our group of nurses. This event is therefore among the least stressful. We also decided to tabulate the numerical differences between the patients' and the nurses' rankings for each event to examine how great the differences in ranking really were. The results of this analysis are shown in Table 5.3.

From this it can be seen, for example, that events 15, 41 and 44 were ranked exactly the same in our study as in the adjusted Volicer & Bohannon work. Similarly, it can be seen that events 17 and 19 were ranked dif-

Table 5.2 Selection of items from Table 5.1 used in Practical 5.1

Assigned rank order from Volicer & Bohannon	Event	Adjusted rank order from Volicer & Bohannon	Rank order from diploma in nursing students
1.	Having strangers sleep in same room with you	1	3
3.	Having to sleep in a strange bed	2	1
6.	Being awakened in the night by the nurse	3	4
8.	Not being able to get newspapers, radio or TV when you want them	4	2
13.	Having to be assisted with a bedpan	5	8
15.	Not having friends visit you	6	6
17.	Thinking your appearance might be changed after your hospitalization	7	13
19.	Thinking you might have pain because of surgery or test procedures	8	14
23.	Being cared for by an unfamiliar doctor	9	5
25.	Not knowing when to expect things will be done to you	10	11
26.	Having the staff be in too much of a hurry	11	7
29.	Having nurses or doctors talk too fast or use words you can't understand	12	10
32.	Knowing you have to have an operation	13	15
35.	Not having your call light answered	14	9
37.	Not having your questions answered by the staff	15	12
40.	Not getting relief from pain medications	16	20
41.	Not knowing the results or reasons for your treatments	17	17
44.	Not being told what your diagnosis is	18	18
46.	Knowing you have a serious illness	19	16
49.	Thinking you might lose your sight	20	19

Table 5.3 Numerical differences in rank ordering of each event between the two samples

	Numerical differences in rank ordering						
	0	1	2	3	4	5	6
Events (identified by	15	3	1	13	23	35	17
Volicer &	41	6	8	37	26		19
Bohannon's	44	25	29	46	40		
assigned ranks		49	32				
from Table 5.2)							
Total	3	4	4	3	3	1	2

ferently by six places and by referring to Table 5.2 it can further be seen that in both cases our sample of nurses ranked them as more stressful than the patients.

Discussion

Perhaps the most pleasing finding is just how good our nurses were at predicting patients' ratings of psychosocial stress. This is even more remarkable when one is reminded that the study is American and that it arose from investigating only medical and surgical patients. Although these events are probably common to a majority of nursing situations, it is possible that the rank ordering will change according to the nursing context under investigation. Our results might reflect the fact that our nurses were all experienced and had been qualified several years. You could test this yourselves by carrying out this practical with student nurses.

Table 5.3 shows where there are discrepancies in the rank ordering. It is interesting to note that our group of nurses felt that patients would be more concerned than they were about any effects on their appearance (event 17). Of more importance is that, whereas our nurses overestimated patients' fears of pain (event 19), they underestimated the stress patients appear to express concerning having calls answered (event 35). This latter finding has important implications for optimizing communication. Although there were some discrepancies in stress ratings concerning being treated by unfamiliar doctors (event 23), staff being in too much of a hurry (event 26) and not getting relief from pain medication (event 40), the differences are not very large.

From this study our results seem to suggest that nurses are more empathic than one would predict from Johnston's study. However, our sample is very small and select and Johnston's study is far more valid in that it was carried out in a ward setting. It would be interesting to carry out this study on larger samples from a wider variety of backgrounds, to see whether our findings can be substantiated. The more empathic nurses are, the better communicators they are likely to become. Perhaps one way of developing empathy is to be a subject in practicals such as this one.

Practical 5.2 Observing group behaviour

Introduction

A very important aspect of interpersonal behaviour is how we behave in group situations, that is with three or more people. Communicating in groups involves both verbal and non-verbal behaviour, although it is probably easier to understand the verbal channel than it is to interpret non-verbal cues. You may, however, be familiar with the idea of non-verbal cues as 'body-language' which has been a popular subject in recent years (cf. Morris 1977).

The topic of communication in small groups is well reviewed by Fraser (1978a, b) who emphasizes structure, leadership, processes of social influence and how effectively groups work. Nurses will be familiar with functioning in all sorts of small groups ranging from the informal to the formal. For example, teaching a group of students on the ward or meeting a group of relatives are usually informal group activities, whereas unit meetings, ward reports, ward rounds and case conferences are often formal structured gatherings. Nurses have to move fairly freely from being group leaders in certain situations to being participants in others, but in all of them they may be required to contribute in some way. Whatever the group situation, it is likely to be a 'real-life' one in which it is difficult to analyse objectively one's own behaviour or gain feedback to improve performance. It is not likely either that a second opportunity will be given to correct a bad performance! In this practical there will be opportunities to try some self-monitoring in situations where mistakes or bad performances do not matter. Though artificial in one sense, they allow time for discussion and to develop self-awareness without the pressure of 'real-life'.

Bales (1950, 1970) has devised an observation schedule for analysing verbal communication in groups. This includes 12 distinct categories into which any utterance can be categorized by trained observers. These categories are subdivided into four broad areas as shown below.

P. Positive reactions
    1. seems friendly
    2. jokes, laughs
    3. agrees

A. Attempted answers
    4. gives suggestion
    5. gives opinion
    6. gives information

Q. Questions
    7. asks for information
    8. asks for opinion
    9. asks for suggestion

N. Negative reactions
    10. disagrees
    11. shows tension
    12. seems unfriendly

It should be emphasized that only minimum account is taken of non-verbal behaviour in this schedule.

As noted previously, while communicating verbally, one is also giving non-verbal cues which serve some communicative function even if it is actually different from the verbal message. A review of communication in the health-care setting by Smith & Bass (1982) has identified a number of functions of non-verbal behaviour. A modified list of these is shown below.

Cp. Complementing: completes, adds to, emphasizes or accents the message.

Ct. Contradicting: when the non-verbal behaviour conflicts with the verbal message, e.g. sarcasm.

R. Regulating: nods, eye contact, etc., to get attention or give cue for somebody else to speak.

S. Substituting: replaces verbal message.

N. Neutral: no clear function.

Such functions are clearly important in analysing group communication.

Method

This practical is divided into two parts. The first is concerned with observing verbal behaviour in groups and the second with interpreting the functions of non-verbal behaviour. We ran these practicals with a group of diploma in nursing students, who took turns at participating in the groups being observed and in acting as observers. It is easier if there are the same number of observers as there are group participants, so that one observer can concentrate on one participant. It is recommended that the group should consist of no more than five members. The idea is that, while the group holds a discussion on a chosen topic, the observers record aspects of their communication on prepared observation schedules. There are two concerned with verbal and two with non-verbal behaviour and it is possible for these to be combined.

Table 5.4 is a modified version of Bales' Interaction Schedule. As you can see, you can put the names of the individuals in the group in the first column. Along the top row are the four broad categories of types of utterance identified by Bales. You may find it helpful for each observer to keep a copy of the 12 distinct categories constituting these four to be referred to during the observation until they are more familiar.

Table 5.4 Schedule for Bales' type analysis of verbal communication in a group.
    1. Frequency and type of utterances

Names	P Positive reactions	A Attempted answers	Q Questions	N Negative reactions	Total
Amanda			1 1	~~1 1 1 1~~	7
Bernard	1	1			2
Carol	1	1 1	1		4
David	1 1 1				3
Elizabeth		1	1		2
Total	5	4	4	5	18

The group is given 3–5 minutes to discuss a particular topic and, as they do so, each observer records the verbal behaviour of a selected group member. Every time the group member starts to speak, the observer decides on the category of the utterance and records it with a stroke, as shown in the Table. This gives measurements for who speaks most (last column) and what kind of utterance category is most common (bottom row).

After this exercise, you might like to try the schedule shown in Table 5.5. Using this schedule you can record who is speaking to whom while coding the nature of the utterance by using its code letter (P, A, Q or N). In a large class, it is possible for the exercise to be carried out by a second group of observers, while the first group of observers does the first exercise. Note that this schedule has a section included for when an individual addresses the whole group. You should always fill in these schedules by working from left to right, such that those in the first column are the initiators of communication, addressing themselves to those on the top row, who are the receivers.

Tables 5.6 and 5.7 are similar, but are concerned with the functions of non-verbal behaviour. Again, it is best to restrict the group to five members and to allocate one person to each individual. You will find it easier if you practise the task using Table 5.6 first and discuss with colleagues how certain behaviours are to be interpreted. Once you have experienced this task you should then use Table 5.7 to give you a more accurate schedule of observation.

Table 5.5 Schedule for Bales' type analysis of verbal communication in a group.
2. Frequency and type of utterances, senders and receivers

Names	Amanda	Bernard	Carol	David	Elizabeth	Group	Total
Amanda	/////	Q	Q N N		N	N N	7
Bernard	A	/////	P				2
Carol	A Q	A	/////		P		4
David			P P	/////	P		3
Elizabeth	Q				/////	A	2
Total	4	2	6	0	3	3	18

Table 5.6 Schedule for Bales' type analysis of non-verbal communication in a group. 3. Frequency and type of cue

Names	Cp	Ct	R	S	N	Total
	Complementing	Contradicting	Regulating	Substituting	Neutral	
Amanda	1 1 1	1 1 1		1	1	8
Bernard		1	1			2
Carol	1	1	1	1	1	5
David	1 1 1					3
Elizabeth		1			1	2
Total	7	5	3	2	3	20

Table 5.7 Schedule for Bales' type analysis of non-verbal communication in a group. 4. Frequency and type of cue, senders and receivers

Names	Amanda	Bernard	Carol	David	Elizabeth	Group	Total
Amanda	////	N	Ct Ct Cp		Ct	Cp S Cp	8
Bernard	Ct	////	R				2
Carol	N S Ct	R	////			Cp	5
David			Cp Cp	////		Cp	3
Elizabeth	N				////	R	2
Total	5	2	6	0	3	4	20

Finally, you should try to observe a group discussing a topic using Tables 5.5 and 5.7. In this task the observers are required to categorize the verbal interaction, who it is addressed to and whether or not there are any accompanying non-verbal cues. Although a very exacting task, the finished product does given an accurate representation of how the group functioned. It is best if the group can be video-taped, so that the observers can record the information at their leisure, although the practical can be carried out spontaneously.

Results

Our data are drawn from one short group discussion lasting about 3 minutes. The topic they were discussing was the 'training of nurses'. We used the same data for Tables 5.4–5.7 to show how they can be analysed fully using these four schedules. To clarify our results we have used fictitious names. It can be seen clearly from the schedules that Amanda tended to dominate the discussion, but in rather a negative way (two questions and five negative reactions). In one instance this person used non-verbal behaviour alone to substitute the verbal message. Bernard participated little in the discussion, unlike Carol, who contributed four verbal utterances, a non-verbal message and was spoken to the most (see Table 5.5, bottom row). David spoke only in a positive way, twice to Carol and once to Elizabeth and nobody addressed a message directly to Elizabeth. Similarly, Elizabeth did not participate a great deal. Finally, the verbal messages were divided approximately equally among the categories, whereas as would be expected, the non-verbal communication was mainly complementing or contradicting.

Discussion

This approach to analysing communication does give quite an accurate picture of what takes place. It does depend, of course, on our observers' reliability, that is their ability to code information under the same categories. With training this can be improved until it is quite efficient. The use of video is extremely helpful in this respect. However, even without video, our groups felt that the schedules did represent what they felt the group had been like. In fact some individuals were surprised that they 'gave so much away', especially through the use of non-verbal cues.

The use of observation schedules in nursing practice is rather an underdeveloped area. One feels it would be a particularly helpful technique to use as part of student training, to help improve communication and develop new strategies. It would also be of value, one suspects, to more experienced nurses, to help them evaluate their own performance in a variety of situations. There are clearly practical limitations on the wide-spread use of observation schedules, but it is crucial to collect this kind of information if communication is to be improved.

The main value of our practical might well be to allow you, as a nurse, to reflect on your own styles of interaction. You might not be aware of the extent to which you, for example, might dominate group discussions, or the nature of the communications you make. Furthermore you might learn more about how your non-verbal behaviour affects the interpretation of your communications. By finding out more about how you normally behave in group situations, you will be in a better position to learn to communicate more effectively. Further aspects of interpersonal communication will be considered in the final practical in this chapter.

Practical 5.3 Perceiving self and others

Introduction

Although the previous practicals may have increased your self-awareness in some respects, it is possible that you have never really seen yourselves as others see you. There are several ways of investigating this sort of question. Initially, we will use two, called 'Portraits' and 'Translation' games as a way of preparing for the third, 'Role play'. The first two were designed by Bannister & Mottram (1973), who have kindly allowed us to reproduce them. The third has been widely used in the behavioural sciences to help people to explore situations from points of view other than their own. All three exercises provide the basis for discussions within groups concerning various aspects of the exercises and the experiences associated with them.

Method

The first part of the practical should be carried out by the class working in pairs. Each partner writes a description of what they are like (a portrait) which they are willing to exchange with their partner. It can be helpful to agree beforehand that comments will be of a constructive nature. This does not mean being uncritical, but the aim is to be helpful. The participants do not necessarily have to know each other well, as early impressions can be explored just as usefully as more long-term ones. Having done their own portrait, each person then writes a portrait of the other person. Finally, a prediction of the portrait written of themselves by the other person should be attempted. The portraits are exchanged and discussed, noting the similarities and differences between them for each person and considering on what 'evidence' the impressions were gained. The implications of the portraits for professional roles should be discussed, as well as any general points which arise.

The second part of the practical can be carried out by the class working in small groups. The numbers in each group do not have to be identical. Translation games are described by Bannister & Mottram (1973) as one of a 'variety of techniques which draw the nurse's attention to the way in which problems are formulated rather than found' (p.18). Each person thinks of their 'best' characteristic, that is one of which they are at least a little proud. They write this down and pass it to the next person, who 'translates' it into a problem, or something which needs to be cured. An example, is that you might consider yourself to be conscientious, which could be translated by others as a cover for the fact that you are really an isolated person who works hard to avoid loneliness. When each person has completed the task, all the translations are discussed in an attempt to analyse how the translations were achieved.

Initially, both parts of the practical can seem a bit threatening, as you decide how much to reveal about yourself and contemplate being confronted with interpretations of your behaviour by your colleagues, as well as their impressions of you. However, there is a sense in which these experiential practicals can increase awareness of how others, especially patients, may feel at having themselves discussed or assessed and it can be revealing to see how your colleagues' impressions of you vary with your impressions of yourself.

Having trusted each other enough to try these practicals, you are probably ready to try role playing, in which your expertise in acting is not the issue. Role play is a way of trying to experience an event from another's point of view and there are all sorts of variations which can be tried.

This practical can be carried out by the whole class. We give 'scripts' for three situations but you can invent your own if you wish. To do this practical, volunteer subjects should each read one or other (not both) of the two scripts for a role play and spend a few minutes thinking themselves into the role. It is important that the players only read their own script and not the one for the other player(s) in the same situation. (All the scripts can be found in Appendix IV.) The rest of the class can read both scripts if they wish. They then observe the enactment of the situation to contribute to a discussion at the end. The players will probably find that their role playing has a natural ending after a few minutes and can stop as soon as they feel they want to.

After each role play, the participants and observers discuss their feelings about the roles they have played, the themes which have emerged, how close it seemed to real life and what professional implications have emerged. You may find the questions in Table 5.8 of assistance to you.

Results and discussion

We spent an afternoon on the three exercises involving 18 diploma in nursing students. In the first two exercises the students gradually warmed to the experience and discussed their findings concerning themselves as professionals. Some found that their colleagues appeared to know them better than they would have guessed, while others were surprised by how different their own perceptions of themselves were compared with others. One group became particularly engrossed in the explanations they developed in the translation game.

The role plays produced some fascinating behaviours. A frequent occurrence was that of constantly deferring to doctors to justify nursing actions. For example, 'the doctor wants you to get up ...' and 'the doctor says you're to have suppositories ...'. Another tendency was to put things

Table 5.8   Considerations to aid in discussion of role playing

Observers (non-verbal interaction and non-verbal cues)

1. Draw up a sketch of what you thought each individual was like as a person
2. Consider where you think certain irretrievable courses of action were chosen. Discuss the outcomes if different approaches had been taken. It may help to play back the role enactment and simply change a decision and see what happens
3. Do you think the needs of each individual were met? Why? (Why not?) What should have happened? Why didn't it?

Players

1. How involved did you feel in your roles and what problems did you encounter in playing them?
2. Are you happy with the outcome? Was it inevitable?

off until later; 'I'll come back later and do it . . .', 'the nurses on the late shift will see to that . . .'. Some players never discovered that, due to the scripting, they were talking at cross-purposes with the patient or doctor and while the audience had the advantage of witnessing this, it was a salutory lesson to the actors when they discovered it. The nurse–doctor relation which emerged from the third role play (C) was in some respects similar to that described by Stein (1975). This paper, called the 'doctor–nurse game', gives a fascinating insight into the manoeuvres made by female nurses to elicit from male doctors the information or behaviour they want without appearing to undermine the doctors' authority.

Other aspects of the analysis of the role play concerned the position and posture of participants, nurses tending to stoop and look down, forcing patients to crane their heads at a funny angle. One sister, trying to get a doctor's attention, could be seen leaning around him into his line of vision as he worked on a venepuncture. The discussions brought to the surface a number of familiar ploys now recognized by nurses for getting their work done and there was great amusement as motives and tactics were revealed and discussed.

The personal or professional value of these exercises is difficult to measure, but an evaluation of the whole afternoon's work is interesting. We asked our students to answer the following questions by giving a score from 1 (not at all) to 5 (a great deal) for each one.

1. Did you learn anything more about yourself and the way people think of you?
2. Did you find the session this afternoon enjoyable?
3. Did you find it interesting?
4. Did you find the session had relevance to your professional role?

Table 5.9 shows the range of scores for each question and indicates that there were many more positive (32 out of 72) than negative (18 out of 72) responses overall. There were 22 out of 72 non-committal responses. The results suggest that, above all, the session was enjoyable but that it was also interesting and of some relevance to the professional role. It was apparently not so helpful from the point of view of learning more about oneself and what others thought.

As noted earlier, these experiential practicals can be threatening, especially where professional standards and behaviours seem to be in question. However, as our evaluation showed, our students found this an enjoyable and rewarding experience in general and, hopefully, it will help them to develop their understanding of themselves and others in future.

Table 5.9 Students' ratings of techniques by using portraits, translation games and role play

Question	Score				
	5	4	3	2	1
1	1	3	4	5	5
2	6	7	4	1	—
3	1	7	7	3	—
4	—	7	7	4	—
Total	8	24	22	13	5
		32		22		18
		(positive)			(negative)	

Conclusion

The focus of this chapter has been on how our perceptions of each other may affect our behaviour toward each other. We investigated nurses' ability to perceive stress in hospital from the patient's point of view and found that they were more empathic than we might have expected. Secondly, we analysed in detail the verbal and non-verbal aspects of small-group communication. If we are able to identify more precisely the nature of these communications, we begin to discover personal styles of communication which could form the basis for improving our own ability to communicate. Finally, we undertook some less structured experiential practicals to compare our perceptions about ourselves with how others see us. In these practicals our students looked at how the meanings we give to ideas can be interpreted in different ways and they investigated the roles of others by playing them.

You will have noticed that in our results and discussion sections we have given you decreasing amounts of data with which to compare your findings. This is one reason why class discussion is so important in these less structured practicals because it goes some way toward ensuring that all possible observations and interpretations are taken into account.

We have pointed out that experiential practicals can be threatening and for this reason, time permitting, we recommend trying them out several times and experimenting with the conditions and situations. We used the examples in this chapter to introduce you to some relevant techniques for nursing but, if you wish to continue improving and monitoring your communication, we recommend your reading Smith & Bass (1982) *Communication for the Health Care Team*, also in this series, as a start.

Summary

In this chapter we emphasized some techniques for measuring and comparing the rather subjective experiences people have about themselves and their situations. In the first practical we used a rank-ordering technique to compare nurses' and patients' perceptions of hospital stresses. In the second, we analysed communication styles in terms of the nature, frequency and direction of utterances and their associated non-verbal cues. The technique here was mainly observation, by using categorized schedules. In the third practical, we used Portraits and Translation games and Role play, which are all relatively unstructured experiential techniques. A simple analysis of our students' reactions to these showed that they enjoyed the session and were generally positive about the experience. Not all investigations of communication have to be as unstructured as some of these. In the next chapter we turn to another technique used by psychologists, experimentation, which demands a much more highly structured controlled approach. This contrasts with the experiential approach and indicates the wide range of possibilities open to us in investigating human behaviour.

References

Argyle, M (1975) *Bodily Communication* London: Methuen

Bales, R F (1950) *Interaction Process Analysis. A Method for the Study of Small Groups* Cambridge, Massachusetts: Addison-Wesley

Bales, R F (1970) *Personality and Interpersonal Behavior* New York: Holt, Rinehart and Winston

Bannister, D & Mottram, K (1973) Teaching psychology to nurses. *Psychology Teaching* **1**, 13–20

Davis, B (1981) Social skills in nursing. In M Argyle (ed.) *Social Skills and Health* London: Methuen

Fraser, C (1978a) Small groups: I. Structure and leadership. In H Tajfel & C Fraser (eds) *Introducing Social Psychology* Harmondsworth: Penguin

Fraser, C (1978b) Small groups: II. Processes and products. In H Tajfel & C Fraser (eds) *Introducing Social Psychology* Harmondsworth: Penguin

Giles, H & Powesland, P F (1975) *Speech Style and Social Evaluation* London: Academic Press

Hargie, O, Saunders, C & Dickson, D (1981) *Social Skills in Interpersonal Communication* London: Croom Helm

Johnston, M (1982) Recognition of patients' worries by nurses and by other patients. *British Journal of Clinical Psychology* **21**, 255–261

Morris, D (1977) *Manwatching: A Field Guide to Human Behaviour* London: Jonathan Cape

Smith, V M & Bass, T A (1982) *Communication for the Health Care Team* London: Harper and Row (Adapted for the UK by A Faulkner)

Stein, L (1975) The doctor–nurse game. In R Dingwall & J McIntosh (eds) *Readings in the Sociology of Nursing* Edinburgh: Churchill Livingstone

Trower, P, Bryant, B & Argyle, M (1978) *Social Skills and Mental Health* London: Methuen

Volicer, B J & Bohannon, M W (1975) A hospital stress rating scale. *Nursing Research* **24**, 352–359

CHAPTER 6

REMEMBERING

How much do patients remember of what their doctor or nurse tells them? Generally people tend to remember the things they are told first (known as the primacy effect) and the things they are told last (the recency effect) better than the things in between (Atkinson & Shiffrin 1971).

Ley & Spelman (1967) found that patients fail to recall 30–50% of what they have been told during consultation with their doctor. Which 50% do the patients actually remember? Ley (1972) found that patients remember best the medical information which they consider to be the most important. They also tend to remember the information which they are given first. However, although patients remember best the things they are told first, the doctor typically gives instructions and advice to them last and the patients consider instructions and advice to be less important than other medical information (Ley 1977). This may contribute to their tendency not to recall the things told to them most recently in the consultation.

The effect of these aspects of memory in patients suggests that they would be unlikely to remember the instructions and advice of the doctor, therefore communication to relieve the patient's condition might not occur, despite the physician actually having told the patient the relevant information. This seems to demonstrate, as Ley (1977) has pointed out, that simply having the will to inform the patient and giving the relevant information will not guarantee effective communication. More understanding is needed of the ways people remember and recall information to maximize effectiveness in communication.

In the situation described, it may be that simply rearranging the order of presentation of information (instructions first) and emphasizing to the patients that which is considered by the doctor to be most important, will enhance the effectiveness of doctor–patient communication. [Ley (1977) tested this and found that, while the patients now recalled more of the instructions and advice, they forgot other statements so that overall the amount of information recalled remained the same.]

Are patients destined only ever to recall 50% of information? Further work suggested to Ley (1977) that the person giving the information can improve total recall by using several strategies. They include using the primacy effect by placing instructions and advice at the start of the information to be presented and stressing how important they are. Other strategies that help include short words and short sentences, being as specific as possible and categorizing or repeating the information. Ley (1979) gives the following example of a general statement compared with a specific one:

> You must lose weight
> You must lost 7lb in weight
> (p.251)

An example of information broken down into categories is given below. It serves to warn the patient first how the information is going to be given, but without at this point giving the actual information. Thus the doctor could say:

> I am going to tell you;
> What is wrong with you;
> What tests we are going to carry out;
> What I think will happen to you;
> What treatment you will need;
> What you must do to help yourself.
> (Ley 1979, p.249)

Having provided the patient with a framework the doctor then proceeds to repeat the categories in the same order, giving the actual details of what is wrong and so on. In this way the doctor is enabling the patient to find ways of organizing the information in a logical order which should help the patient to remember it after the consultation.

Can this type of research be applied to nursing? Clark & Hockey (1979) make a plea for nurses to be prepared to research all aspects of communication, as 'communication is central to the practice of nursing' (p.96). There are numerous situations in which nurses are asked to give information. Some of them may have considerable importance for the patients and their recovery. For example, studies of preoperative information-giving (Hayward 1975; Boore 1978) suggest that patients given specific information require less postoperative analgesia than those given none.

Faulkner (1980) has categorized the information patients ask from nurses into four main groups:

concerning service arrangements (e.g. meal times, etc.);
concerning areas of interest (e.g. nurses' off duty);
concerning treatments (e.g. drugs);
concerning the illness (e.g. diagnosis, prognosis).

In the case of treatments, many studies have shown that a problem exists known as non-compliance, when, for some reason, patients fail to carry out instructions or complete courses of treatment (Ley 1977). It is also the case that health professionals do not themselves comply with advice about patient care (Ley 1981). If this problem can be related to memory, and Ley & Spelman (1967) believe it can, nurses could play an important role: for example, it is often nurses who hand over drugs and instructions to patients when they leave hospital. Understanding of the ways patients remember information could help nurses to ensure that the instructions they give are effectively communicated to the patient.

The following simple experiments are designed to help you gain some understanding of memory and recall. They deal with normal healthy individuals, not patients, therefore one must consider how being a patient might affect the results of the experiments; for example, could stress or anxiety make memory worse, or better? Would physical illness affect memory differently from mental illness? The experiments are first steps in understanding some aspects of memory and recall.

Practical 6.1 Experiment to investigate the effect of serial position on recall

Introduction

This experiment is designed to investigate whether the position of items of information in a particular communication affects how well they are recalled. As we have seen in the introduction to the chapter the possibility that it does has implications for people in the health-care setting; patients may remember most of the information they are given and enhance their recovery or adaptation to a condition if staff are able to take advantage of this factor. Similarly, nurses might be able to enhance their own ability to teach other nurses and organize their own learning more effectively.

Method

This experiment takes a matter of minutes to complete. It can be carried out by a tutor using the class as subjects or students can collect data among themselves. We used a class of 14 first-year degree nurses. The experimenter will need a watch with a second hand; the subjects each need a pencil and paper. In Appendix V there is a list of 15 anatomical items (List A) which only the experimenter should look at. The subjects are given the following instructions:

> I am going to read a list of 15 words. You should try to memorize them all. You will then have 45 seconds to write down as many words as you can remember, in any order.

The experimenter then reads the list clearly, one word every 2 seconds. The 45-second period is then timed.

Results

To speed up the scoring the list of words should be read out again in the same order and the subjects should indicate each word successfully recalled. The order they are recalled in does not matter. The results are charted as shown in Table 6.1 and the percentage recall rate is obtained by dividing the number of responses for a particular word by the number in the group and multiplying by 100. Thus word number 1 scored 10 correct responses; the percentage recall rate is then $(10/14) \times 100 = 71.4\%$. Numbers are rounded down or up to the nearest whole number depending on whether the fraction is smaller or greater than 0.5. In this case it was

Table 6.1 Serial position and percentage recall rate (number of students = 14)

Word position	1	2	3	4	5	6	7	8	9	10	11	12	13	14	15
Correct responses	10	14	11	10	8	6	3	4	7	4	6	5	10	8	10
Recall rate (%)	71	100	78	71	57	42	21	28	50	28	42	35	71	57	71

0.4 and rounded down to 71%. The results should then be drawn on to a graph as shown in Figure 6.1. In this Figure the continuous line corresponds to the percentage recall rates attained by our group of students.

Discussion

Our results support the idea that people tend to remember the things they are told first (the primacy effect) and the things they are told last (the recency effect) better than the things in between. Figure 6.1 indicates clearly the presence of primacy and recency effects in which recall is seen to be better at the beginning and end of the test, and worse in the middle. (The broken line indicates a typical graph of such effects for comparison.) Our graph, however, has an unexpected peak at position 9. This corresponds with the word 'pleura' and the students thought the reason for this being recalled so well in the middle of the task might be related to a lecture earlier in the week on the respiratory system. This happened by chance, but you could test it yourself by substituting a very familiar word or name in place of one of the others in the list and retesting another group of students. Alternatively use the same students but make up a new list.

As we saw at the beginning of the chapter, Ley (1977) has tried to make use of this kind of practical knowledge in health-care settings. You may well find opportunities in your own work to observe or implement this kind of strategy. Another example of how to help patients recall more information suggested by Ley (1979) was to organize the information in some way. He used categories to divide up the information a doctor might need to give a patient. In the next experiment we will investigate a very simple form of organization and measure its effect on recall.

Practical 6.2 Experiment to investigate the effect of organization on the recall of unrelated words

Introduction

This experiment is designed to investigate whether subjects given instructions to organize their learning will be able to recall a greater number of words than those subjects not given any assistance. To do this it will be necessary to have two conditions, one in which a group of students will

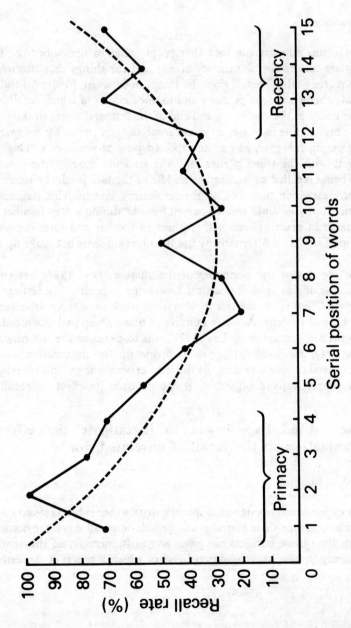

Figure 6.1 Graph of percentage recall rate against serial position, showing primacy and recency effects.
—— % recall rates attained; - - - predicted recall rates.

be given instructions on how to organize the information, and another in which no such information will be given.

Method

This experiment can be carried out by a tutor and a class of subjects or by students themselves collecting data from friends or colleagues. We used a class of 14 first-year degree nurses. At least three individuals including the experimenter are needed, but it is better if more can be involved. There are two conditions, but it does not matter if there are not identical numbers in each. You will need a watch with a second hand and 11 response slips and a pencil for each subject. (See Appendix VI for sample response slips.) Subjects are randomly assigned into two groups: one group, recognized by the letters 'CS' (control subjects), will simply be instructed to continue the task; the other which is the experimental group, 'ES', will be given further instructions on how to organize the task. For the first three trials both groups are given the same instructions so that baseline data can be obtained.

Before the experiment the experimenter should write each word from List B (to be found in Appendix VI) on a separate card so that the words can be shuffled and read out in a random order. The subjects should not see the words before the start of the experiment.

The subjects are given the following instructions:

> I am going to read out a list of 24 words. You should try to memorize them all. At the end of each trial you will be given 1 minute to write down as many words as you can remember on a fresh slip of paper. You should write the number of the trial at the top of each response slip. When you have finished writing or the minute is up turn your response slip face down and write the next trial number on the next slip. I will then read the list again and the same procedure will be repeated.

The experimenter reads the words at approximately 2-second intervals and shuffles them thoroughly between each trial.

After the first three trials for collecting baseline data, the conditions are changed. In Appendix VI, there are two sets of instructions, one for group 'CS' and one for group 'ES'. After the first three trials these instructions are given to the groups such that neither group knows what the other instructions are. The experiment is continued for a further eight trials under the new conditions. It is vital that subjects remember to number each response slip according to the number of each trial.

Results

The total number of words recalled by each subject for each trial is calculated. A quick way to do this is for each person to be responsible for collecting say, all the scores for the first trial, someone else all the scores for the second trial and so on, within each group. These can then be entered onto a master score sheet as shown in Table 6.2. The mean score per trial is then calculated. Thus, for trial 1, subjects in the 'CS' group scored $11 + 9 + 11 + 10 + 10 + 8 + 13 = 72$. This is divided by the number of subjects in the group, 7, giving a mean score of 10.3. This is rounded to the nearest whole number, 10. Finally the mean scores for each trial are plotted on a graph. Use two colours or broken vs continuous lines to represent the two groups. Our results are shown in Figure 6.2.

Discussion

The experimental group 'ES' was instructed to use the alphabet to help recall of the 24 items. There was one item per letter of the alphabet excepting for X and Z. Although the experimental group (ES) showed a decline in recall on first being given the organization instructions, a rapid recovery leading to enhanced recall as compared with the control group (CS) was shown. When asked about the reasons for the drop in performance on trial 4, the subjects related this to thinking about the alphabet and having to apply it to the task. Having spent one or two trials assimilating the instructions they were then able to achieve improved recall as compared with the control group.

Our results then indicate that providing some kind of simple strategy to help subjects remember information can improve recall. You may be able to think of ways of using this knowledge yourself in your work. One example that may be familiar is to use the four letters at the beginning of the alphabet to recall priorities in cardiac arrest or first-aid procedures. As Ley (1979) has shown it does not have to be just the alphabet which is used and you may well be able to invent aids yourself depending on your specific circumstances. In the next experiment we look at further aspects of memory by investigating the role of recognition compared with recall in presenting information to people.

Table 6.2 Mean scores on each trial for control and experimental groups

| Trial | Control (n = 7) Subject no. | | | | | | | | Experimental (n = 7) Subject no. | | | | | | | |
	1	2	3	4	5	6	7	Mean	8	9	10	11	12	13	14	Mean
1	11	9	11	10	10	8	13	10	9	10	11	7	12	10	12	10
2	11	10	14	11	14	12	15	12	11	11	13	10	16	11	12	12
3	13	11	15	13	15	12	15	13	11	13	14	11	17	15	11	13
4	14	10	12	15	12	12	14	13	12	12	11	12	10	8	7	10
5	17	16	13	12	14	17	13	14	14	13	9	16	14	9	19	13
6	17	11	13	16	12	13	16	14	15	11	18	15	12	17	17	15
7	13	13	15	17	13	16	11	14	11	16	17	15	8	15	14	14
8	18	14	20	13	19	16	16	16	23	21	15	21	20	15	20	19
9	14	18	13	14	18	15	21	16	23	21	20	16	19	20	16	19
10	15	17	13	14	18	15	20	15	22	21	19	18	21	21	16	19
11	15	18	14	14	18	15	20	16	22	21	18	19	21	21	17	20

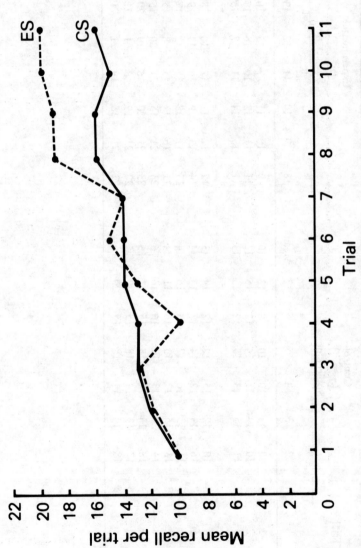

Figure 6.2 Graph to show effect of organization on recall as compared with no organization. ES, Experimental subjects; CS, control subjects.

Practical 6.3 Experiment to compare recall with recognition

Introduction

This experiment is designed to investigate whether it is easier to recall information or to recognize it. Generally, it appears that recognition, in which we have to identify information from material presented to us, is easier than recall, where we have to actually retrieve an item from our memory. If this is the case, it has important implications for nursing, as it is often nurses who give patients information about prescribed medications or rehabilitation to be continued at home away from medical or nursing supervision.

Method

This experiment that takes a matter of minutes to complete can either be carried out by the tutor using the class as subjects or the students can collect data themselves from nursing friends or colleagues. (Students do not need more than four people to co-operate.) We recorded data from a class of 14 first-year degree nurses. Subjects are randomly divided into two groups (recognition vs recall), although it does not matter if there are different numbers in each group. From List C (Appendix VII) the experimenter(s) should construct a list of 10 drugs, for example, Dromoran, Aludrox SA, Inderal, Pethilorfan, Mogadon, Lasix, Omnopon, Ventolin, Dulcolax and Dexedrine.

First of all the subjects are given this list and then they are given the following instructions:

> Here is a list of drugs. You have 45 seconds in which to memorize them. You will then be tested to see how well you have done.

After this the 'Recognition' group is given List C and asked to underline those drugs which were in the original list. The 'Recall' group is given a sheet of paper and asked to write down the drugs in any order.

Results

One mark is awarded to each drug correctly recalled or recognized. This information should be entered on a sheet as shown (Table 6.3). In the recall condition, a mark should only be awarded if the experimenter is

Table 6.3   Data comparing recall with recognition

Recall condition			Recognition condition		
Subject no.	Correct	Errors	Subject no.	Correct	Errors
1	3	1	8	10	—
2	2	—	9	10	—
3	4	3	10	9	—
4	3	2	11	9	1
5	5	—	12	8	—
6	3	1	13	10	—
7	2	2	14	7	—
Total	25	9		63	1

sure that the drug can be recognized and that the subject is certain which drug is being referred to. In our study, for example, we marked 'Dorawan' incorrect but 'Lasex' correct. You might wish to be more strict and only score correct those drugs recalled exactly. A simple way to analyse these results to give some indication of the significance is to compare the mean scores of the total number correct for each condition. In our example we can see that the mean score for the recall condition (25/7) = 3.6 (which is rounded up to 4, the nearest whole number) is much lower than that for the recognition condition which is (63/7) = 9.

This seems to suggest that recognition is easier than recall. The recognition group also made fewer errors, only one compared with nine in the recall group.

Discussion

These results are of considerable interest to nurses given that people are quite likely to forget details when asked simply to recall them. When giving information to patients, for example, it may be considered necessary to present it in written form to help them to remember it rather than to rely on their recall abilities.

Nurses need to consider how their own ability to recall important information might be affected at times. For example, the principle that nurses never take verbal or telephone messages for drugs to be given to patients applies here. The experiment demonstrates how accuracy is reduced in recall situations and supports the need for written instructions. If under stress or distracted when treating a patient, it is possible that recall will be affected even more. This suggestion could be investigated by your designing a further experiment to measure the effects of say, distraction on recall and recognition.

An interesting consideration in relation to this experiment is exactly what is being tested when multiple-choice questions are asked as, for example, in nursing examinations. This is more a recognition test than one of recall, although both processes are involved. It might be argued that recall questions are better to show the unforced errors people make. As can be seen from our data, the recall condition produced a number of unrelated errors which for nursing could indeed prove to be very serious.

We should, however, be a little cautious in interpreting our data. By using a 'between-subjects' design we do not know whether subjects in the recognition group simply had better memories. This would need further testing by a 'within-subjects' design or by matching the groups for their ability to memorize. Another factor is that the material used is relatively familiar to nurses and this may well have affected the results. This may be important in several ways. Is a person most likely to make errors with familiar material by being slightly over-confident, or could unfamiliarity with material make remembering it more difficult and therefore lead to errors? You may like to design experiments of your own now to try and test questions such as these.

Conclusion

From these three experiments it can be seen that the way in which we present information to people affects how they remember it. The first experiment demonstrates the well known primacy and recency effects. In the nursing situation there may well be other factors which influence whether patients are better able to recall the information which is presented at the beginning and the end. If, for example, they do not understand the information being given them they may 'switch-off' at an early stage and simply stop listening. On the other hand, they may have to concentrate so hard to understand the first part of the message that the latter information is not coded or understood. Clearly, we must be careful in using our knowledge of memory processes in the work situation and not assume that every experimental finding will automatically be transferable. They should, however, give us some insights into how best to prepare ourselves and our patients when giving them information.

This was well illustrated in the second and third experiments. Here we imposed strategies to help our subjects remember better. In the second task they used the alphabet to help organize a list of words to be recalled. As an organizing strategy it worked very well and it may be that we should give more thought to how we organize the information we expect patients to remember.

Similarly, we found that our subjects could recognize more than they could recall. This does strengthen the argument for giving more written information to patients relatives and colleagues, provided that it is specific and expressed in an appropriate way. One suspects that in a busy hospital ward we rely too much on what we tell people to do and very rarely check whether we have communicated our message effectively. Hopefully this chapter will have helped you in your task of giving information to others by having made you more aware of some of the practical aspects of remembering.

Summary

In this chapter we have introduced the reader to some important research about remembering. Special emphasis was given in the introduction to the pioneering work of Ley and his colleagues. Three experiments made up the practical work in this chapter, all of which were designed to illustrate some of the many factors affecting remembering. The implications of these were discussed and some suggestions made to help nurses in their everyday work.

References

Atkinson, R C & Shiffrin, R M (1971) The control of short-term memory. *Scientific American* **225**, 82–90

Boore, J R P (1978) *Prescription for Recovery.* London: Royal College of Nursing

Clark, J M & Hockey, L (1979) *Research for Nursing: a Guide for the Enquiring Nurse* Aylesbury: HM & M

Faulkner, A (1980) Communication and the nurse. *Nursing Times Occasional Papers* **76**, 93–95

Hayward, J (1975) *Information – A Prescription against Pain* London: Royal College of Nursing

Ley, P (1972) Complaints made by the hospital staff and patients: a review of the literature. *Bulletin of the British Psychological Society* **25**, 115–120

Ley, P (1977) Psychological studies of doctor–patient communication. In S Rachman (ed.) *Contributions to Medical Psychology* vol. I. Oxford: Pergamon

Ley, P (1979) Memory for medical information. *British Journal of Social and Clinical Psychology* **18**, 245–255

Ley, P (1981) Professional non-compliance: a neglected problem. *British Journal of Clinical Psychology* **20**, 151–154

Ley, P & Spelman, M (1967) *Communicating with the Patient* London: Staples

CHAPTER 7

THE WORK SITUATION

In Chapter 2 we looked at personality and some of the various factors which have been measured in people who choose nursing as their career. We pointed out that much of the research in this area resulted from concern at the 'wastage' problem, that is the high drop-out rates among nurses. A similar problem is sickness absenteeism and the two are often investigated simultaneously as 'absence and wastage' (e.g. Clark & Redfern 1978a, b). Although there have been hopeful signs of a decline in the proportion of student nurses leaving training before qualifying (DHSS 1982), a more recent note in *Nursing Times* (1983) points to a worsening of the problem again. There have been several large-scale reviews and surveys related to these problems (cf. Clark & Redfern 1978a, b; Redfern 1978; Moores *et al.* 1982) and numerous articles and discussion papers. They have tried to define, measure and explain the nature of the problem and to identify the causes. In so doing they have focused on issues such as the quality of working life, job satisfaction, stresses in nursing and occupational expectations.

According to Smith (1981) the quality of working life is affected by the interaction between the goals of individuals and the goals of the organization in which they work. This is similar to the idea described in Chapter 2, that individuals choose a career which is thought to reflect their personal needs and values. Thus many health-care professionals may have perceived their chosen professions as providing them with opportunities to meet their need to work with and help people. If the goals of the individual and the organization differ, problems can arise. For example, if as a nurse one of your goals is to provide emotional support for patients which involves spending time talking with them, but the orientation of your ward sister is to complete the day's work according to a set regimen gauged by the clock, your quality of working life may be negatively affected.

Job satisfaction is a term often used in association with studies of the quality of working life; it describes a state that depends not only on workers' commitment to their work but also on aspects of the work situation, such as colleague relations, pay, conditions and prospects. Job satisfaction is described by Berns (1982) as a subordinate to life satisfaction and therefore also dependent on factors outside the working environment such as home life, family relations and outside interests.

In this chapter we are going to consider some of these issues. Whether or not one is considering leaving nursing, factors relating to the quality of working life are probably important to all nurses. At the simplest level it seems likely that nurses who are satisfied with their work may choose to stay and may perhaps feel able to give better care to patients and others than those who feel distressed, discontented or are repeatedly absent.

We know that many nurses leave nursing and that others express dissatisfaction at times. What is not so clear is exactly what causes these feelings. We will look at a small sample of studies which may give some clues, though it must be emphasized that we do not intend to try and cover all the possible issues.

Practical 7.1 An investigation into nurses' self-perceptions and the public's image of the typical nurse

Introduction

Role conflict in nursing has been investigated by Murray (1983) who compared nurses' self-image with how they thought the public viewed them. He took a cross-section of all grades of nurse from first-year students to ward sisters in a large sample of 246. In his study Murray asked the nurses to score themselves on a series of rating scales assessing professional, traditional and personality dimensions. He then asked them to complete the same scales according to how they thought the public saw them. It was found that the student nurses saw themselves rather differently from the image they thought the public held of them. This discrepancy was described as a form of 'role conflict'. He related this finding to the substantial proportion of nurses in his study who had experienced a desire to leave nursing. The nurses who felt the most conflict were second- and third-year students. Experienced nurses did not express the same degree of conflict and first-year nurses experienced it less than other students.

We are going to use Murray's rating scales (see Table 7.1) in this practical to replicate part of Murray's study and to develop it in one respect (in his study Murray did not collect any data showing what the public actually thinks nurses are like). This will enable us to see whether nurses' beliefs about the image they think the public holds is similar to the image the public actually holds and whether the image held by nurses of themselves differs from that held by the public. These are clearly important variables in understanding role conflict in nursing.

Method

This practical can be carried out by the whole class. We involved our class of 19 experienced nurses taking the Diploma in Nursing and collected further data ourselves from the public. Each class member should complete the scales shown in Table 7.1 as instructed. After having described yourself on these scales you should then fill them in according to what you think the public expects you to be like. This will enable you to see whether there is any conflict between how you see yourselves and how you think others see you.

Having done this you should then organize yourselves to collect information from members of the general public. It may be quicker if some class members analyse the data already collected while the remainder contact members of the public. To avoid the problems of bias you should not let your subjects know you are nurses. If they did know they might try to give you answers that are socially desirable. In selecting members of the public it might be better to move right away from a hospital setting, to a shopping centre for example. As with all the data you collect, the members of the public approached should have the nature of the project briefly explained to them and be invited to take part on the understanding that their participation is voluntary and anonymous. A suitable introduction might be:

> Excuse me, I wonder if you have a moment to help me with a small project about nurses? I am asking members of the public to fill in this rating scale describing the typical nurse to find out how the public views nurses. It is completely anonymous and will only take a few minutes.

Table 7.1 Scales to assess role conflict in nursing (Murray 1983)

Below are a series of word-opposites that you can use to describe nurses. To do this you have to tick the number on each word-opposite which you think best describes yourself. For example, if you are very small you would tick 1 in this word-opposite.

	1	2	3	4	5	
Small						Big

If you are quite big you would tick 4, and if you are of medium build you would tick 3.

Now describe yourself with the following word-opposites.

	1	2	3	4	5	
Shy						Confident
Sympathetic						Unsympathetic
Selfish						Generous
Clumsy						Skilful
Clever						Dim
Talkative						Quiet
Warm						Cold
Competent						Incompetent
Dour						Cheerful
Romantic						Practical
Self-willed						Submissive
Delicate						Healthy
Careless						Careful
Attractive						Plain
Friendly						Unfriendly
Lazy						Industrious
Gentle						Harsh
Dull						Lively
Knowledgeable						Ignorant
Happy						Unhappy
Disorganized						Organized
Hot-headed						Cool-headed
Efficient						Inefficient
Tidy						Untidy
	1	2	3	4	5	

Murray, M (1983) Role conflict and intention to leave nursing. *Journal of Advanced Nursing* 8, 29–31.
Reprinted with the kind permission of the author.

You will need to change the instructions included in the rating scale shown in Table 7.1 when you use it for the public. After your subject has completed the task you should explain a bit more about the project. You should tell your subject that you are a nurse yourself and that you intend comparing the different ways nurses describe themselves with the public's image. Any questions should be answered as they arise. For our sample we matched the subjects approximately by age and kept a similar sex ratio with the group of diploma in nursing students who had rated themselves. We had 16 subjects in all in our sample from the general public and it is likely that they were fairly select and that their knowledge of nurses was largely drawn from their experiences of becoming a parent as they were drawn primarily from a local playgroup. You might like to select a more representative sample for your study, although often it is easier to focus on a specific group of people.

Results

As in previous practicals we calculated the mean score for each scale for the nurses' image of themselves, for how they thought the general public viewed them and for a select sample of the general public. This data is shown in Table 7.2. Murray (1983) in his paper organized the scales according to three dimensions: professional, personality and traditional. Professional refers to those qualities associated with specialized knowledge and skills, whereas traditional covers those qualities associated with loving care. The personality dimension is similar to the traditional, although it is seen as focusing more specifically on attributes of personality. We have followed this pattern to make it easier for you to compare our results and your results with those of Murray's original work.

Discussion

The first important finding is that our results were very similar to those obtained by Murray with his much bigger sample. There appears to be a conflict between nurses' self-image and how they think the public view them in almost every instance. It is clear that nurses believe that the public expect a great deal from them and, although their own self-image is quite high, this does not match their expectations. This potential conflict is clearly a topic worth investigating further and as Murray suggests might well be related to the wastage problem.

It is our second major finding, however, that makes these results even

Table 7.2 Mean scores for nurses' self-image, perceived public-image and actual public-image

Scale	Mean scores		
1–5	Self-image	Perceived public-image	Actual public-image
Professional dimension			
Clumsy–skilful	4.0	4.6	3.8
Clever–dim	2.4	1.9	2.5
Competent–incompetent	1.7	1.2	2.0
Careless–careful	4.1	4.8	4.5
Lazy–industrious	4.0	4.8	3.7
Knowledgeable–ignorant	2.4	1.8	2.1
Disorganized–organized	3.6	4.3	3.8
Efficient–inefficient	2.2	1.2	1.9
Traditional dimension			
Shy–confident	3.5	4.8	4.4
Talkative–quiet	2.5	2.5	2.6
Warm–cold	2.0	1.5	2.3
Delicate–healthy	4.7	4.7	4.2
Friendly–unfriendly	1.7	1.5	2.1
Dull–lively	4.3	4.0	3.8
Happy–unhappy	1.9	1.5	2.2
Personality dimension			
Sympathetic–unsympathetic	1.8	1.2	2.6
Selfish–generous	3.6	4.4	3.6
Dour–cheerful	4.0	4.6	4.3
Romantic–practical	3.5	4.8	3.9
Self-willed–submissive	2.2	2.5	2.2
Attractive–plain	3.0	2.4	2.9
Gentle–harsh	2.1	1.5	2.4
Tidy–untidy	2.4	1.4	2.0

more interesting. In all three cases the actual public-image is either equidistant from the other two mean scores or is more like the nurses' own self-image. In fact the latter finding holds for 17 of the scales. The three exceptions are careless–careful, shy–confident and dull–lively. These findings do suggest that the public-image of nurses is lower than nurses think it is.

This practical raises a number of issues concerning the work situation. It would be particularly useful to replicate our study with a much larger sample to see if we obtain the same results. However, if it is the case that nurses overestimate what others think of them this clearly can pose problems in the work situation. It rather suggests that nurses might be evaluating their job satisfaction using unrealistic criteria which are in fact too demanding. What is quite surprising is just how congruent the self-image of the nurses we used for our study was with the actual public-image. Where there are differences is particularly interesting. Nurses do appear to feel less confident than the public rate them. On the other hand, they consider themselves to be healthier and more lively than the public view of them. Perhaps the most important difference is that nurses do consider themselves to be more sympathetic than the public think they are. This gives further support to the finding that the group of nurses we used has a particularly high self-concept.

This study suggests that we ought to investigate this issue in more detail. We need to collect more data from a much wider cross-section of the public. Age and sex might be important factors affecting the results. We should also find out whether there are any differences between those of the general public who have been hospitalized and the rest. The final point is that in a general sense we do need to know more about what people, especially patients, expect of nurses. This is a very important consideration in coming to a better understanding of the nurses' work situation.

Practical 7.2 An investigation into stresses in nursing

Introduction

In the previous practical stress arising from perceived role conflict was related to discontent within nursing and the possibility of nurses leaving the profession. In Practical 7.2 we are going to consider some specific factors associated with the work which nurses do. First, we will look briefly at two studies of stress in nursing, which have considered the problem from differing perspectives. The first by Parkes (1980a, b) is one of a number of studies (cf. Tomlin 1977; Wallace 1982) which have investigated whether some types of nursing are particularly stressful (e.g. intensive therapy, medical or surgical nursing) compared with others. The second, by Nichols et al. (1981), is similar but concluded that it is not the type of nursing which causes stress, but the psychosocial aspects of the work environment such as whether or not the staff support each other which are important. The term stress is often used to describe a variety of negative experiences such as anxiety, anger, unhappiness and discontent, and we will also use it in this rather non-specific sense.

Parkes (1980a, b) investigated occupational stress among student nurses in a longitudinal study of medical and surgical, male and female wards. Her studies showed that raised stress levels were not always associated with a drop in work satisfaction. For example, surgical wards and male wards were associated with increases in stress but also greater work satisfaction. Medical wards, on the other hand, were associated with increases in stress but also greater work satisfaction. Medical wards, on the other hand, were associated with increases in stress but decreases in work satisfaction. Female wards were found to be less stressful but also less satisfying. It may be that the acquisition of those technical skills required in the surgical ward is more rewarding to students in their first year than the demand for interpersonal skills on medical wards which they may at that stage feel incapable of mastering. A further point of interest in this study was that sickness absenteeism was the same regardless of the levels of stress and work satisfaction. This is interesting because stress and dissatisfaction are sometimes thought to provoke increases in sickness absence. The finding of particular interest to us though is that situational factors (e.g. surgical nursing) can be related to stress in student nurses.

Another type of nursing that has received attention as it is thought to be a high-stress area is intensive therapy. It seems likely that intensive nursing of the critically ill, possibly dying patient, surrounded by machinery and demanding high levels of concentration, would be very stressful for nurses, leading perhaps to discontent and dissatisfaction. Nichols et al. (1981) conducted studies of distress and discontent in nurses in eight intensive therapy units, comparing them with two renal, one medical and one surgical unit. The results were surprising in showing high levels of job satisfaction in the intensive therapy units. Those features of the work that were criticized by the nurses were not those found only in intensive therapy units but the psychosocial factors which could be found in any work situation. The study was therefore taken by the authors to indicate the types of factors which can make nurses unhappy in their work regardless of the type of nursing involved. These include the availability of support, feedback on performance, the management of mistakes made by nurses, and the quality of staff relations. This final point partly reflects the comment made in the Briggs report (1972) that care begins with the relations between nurses, although Nichols et al. also included relations with medical staff in their study.

We have designed this practical to help you investigate some of the causes of stress in nursing and specifically to try and discover whether nurses are more stressed by psychosocial or by situational factors. The practical is based on the method used by Holmes & Rahe (1967) to identify and measure stressful life events and explained briefly in Chapter 3. A similar technique will be used to try and identify what kinds of events cause stress to nurses at work. There are two stages, one in which you identify various stress factors and assign an arbitrary starting score to one of them, and the second in which other people rate these so that they can be ordered according to the degree of stress they cause nurses.

Method

This practical can be carried out by the whole class. We divided our 19 diploma in nursing students into two groups so they could each design a scale for the other group to complete. It took most of an afternoon to design the scales, administer them, score and analyse them. You could cut down the time by designing the scales together, then letting people complete them in their spare time, collecting them for analysis later.

The first thing to do in your groups is 'brainstorm', that is on the basis of your experience as nurses make a list of ideas about factors which you think cause stress in nursing. These should be sorted into two sections, psychosocial (likely to be present in any nursing environment) and situational (found only in specific types of nursing). A final list of about 15–20 items should be compiled with roughly equal numbers in each section. One item, regarded as likely to be typical for all nurses but not especially stressful, should be assigned an arbitrary score of say 250 points (see item 8 in Table 7.3 and item 1 in Table 7.4). The scale is then ready to be presented to the other group of your sample of subjects. The subjects should be asked to consider each item individually according to whether it is perceived as more or less stressful than the item scored 250. They should be further instructed to award each item a score according to the extent to which it is more or less stressful than the item already rated. For simplicity subjects should score in multiples of 10. Tables 7.3 and 7.4 show the lists compiled by our two groups. The items are presented within their sections for clarity, but it may be wise to present the items in a random order to your colleagues to try and avoid bias.

Table 7.3   Items (1–15) selected as stressful to nurses at work: group I

	Pyschosocial	
1	difficulty with off-duty	
2	inability to cope with situations/crises	
3	difficult patients/relatives	
4	conflict in approach to care	
5	lack of resources/staff	
6	lack of support/recognition from managers/peers	
7	lack of understanding/recognition from other disciplines	
8	fluctuations in patient turnover	... 250 points
	Situational	
9	working with much technical equipment	
10	caring for patients out of context of the environment they should be in	
11	dealing with patients with overdose	
12	coping with terminal illness	
13	uncertainity whether to resuscitate	
14	going to too many meetings	
15	working with high death rate	

Psychosocial, likely to occur in any nursing environment; situational, likely to be specific to particular types of nursing.

Results

Our results are shown in Table 7.5 for group I and in Table 7.6 for group II. You should make similar master sheets for your results. Each item's total score was calculated by adding together the scores given by each student. To find out the rank order of the items (from most to least stressful) we gave the item with the highest total score a rank of one, and worked through the list. To find out whether psychosocial or situational factors were more stressful to nurses, we calculated the subtotal for all the items in each section. There were uneven numbers of items in each section, therefore to find the more stressful section, the mean score was obtained by dividing the subtotal for the section by the number of items in that section. These results are shown in Table 7.7. In the case of group I, this indicated that psychosocial factors were considered as being more stressful than situational factors. This was despite the fact that the two most stressful items (item 12, coping with terminal illness, and item 15,

Table 7.4   Items (1–15) selected as stressful to nurses at work: group II

Psychosocial

1	having to do shift work	... 250 points
2	interference with social life	
3	lack of communication with other disciplines	
4	feelings of inadequacy in unfamiliar situations	
5	personal problems affecting work	
6	dealing with relatives	
7	lack of adequate back-up services	
8	need to maintain unnatural attitudes toward others (professional façade)	

Situational

9	dilemmas over resuscitation
10	autocratic attitudes of medical officers
11	dealing with the dying
12	staff shortages
13	equipment shortages
14	working in isolation
15	environmental hazards (e.g. dogs on the district)

Psychosocial, likely to occur in any nursing environment; situational, likely to be specific to particular types of nursing.

working with high death rate) were situational factors. Group II obtained the opposite result from group I, with situational factors being rated as more stressful than psychosocial.

Discussion

From Table 7.7 we can see that the differences between the mean score for each section are really quite small: we are comparing means of 2584 with 2490 in group I and 1924 with 2057 in group II. The nurses seem to perceive the two types of stresses as only marginally different. One reason for this may be the nature of the wording of the items included in the list. The scales may not have distinguished clearly enough between the psychosocial and the situational factors. On the other hand of course, it may be that neither type of factor is really more important than the other, despite the findings of Parkes (1980a, b) and Nichols *et al.* (1981) which suggest that they could be. To try and test the validity of your list you would have to try it out on different groups of nurses.

Table 7.5   Master sheet of scores obtained by each item: group I

Item	Student no.										Total	Rank
	1	2	3	4	5	6	7	8	9	10		
Psychosocial factors												
1	100	140	100	100	150	200	100	100	20	40	1050	14
2	300	360	300	350	150	380	500	260	30	300	2930	5
3	280	340	400	150	30	430	300	310	350	70	2660	7
4	400	440	350	200	400	370	470	400	250	100	3380	3
5	150	340	350	250	100	450	490	380	300	120	2930	5
6	100	300	400	50	500	210	480	350	10	140	2640	8
7	290	400	420	300	70	130	370	150	300	150	2580	9
8	250	250	250	250	250	250	250	250	250	250	2500	10
Situational factors												
9	30	200	350	300	20	100	150	50	350	50	1600	13
10	400	150	200	350	100	100	420	280	50	300	2350	11
11	180	140	400	50	400	150	200	120	100	350	2190	12
12	320	500	500	450	450	300	310	300	300	400	3830	1
13	200	550	450	450	50	380	450	20	100	500	3000	4
14	170	100	100	150	10	120	50	10	100	150	960	15
15	310	480	480	400	260	350	400	70	300	450	3500	2

In addition to these results, we can also use the findings to look at the scoring of each item by individual students (by reading across Table 7.5 or 7.6). For group I (Table 7.5) we can see that there is often a wide range of scores for each item and that therefore the nurses do not perceive the stresses in exactly the same way. For example, item 6 (lack of support/recognition from managers/peers) has scores ranging from 10 to 500. For some nurses this is obviously not perceived as a problem at all, but for others it is the worst problem. We can work out an individual nurse's profile for these stresses by reading down the columns; we could, for example, compare scores of student no. 5 with those of student no. 9 to see if they have a different pattern of responses. The worst stresses for student no. 9 are items 3 (difficult patients/relatives) and 9 (working with much technical equipment) which were scored 350, whereas student no. 5 has scored the same items as among the lowest stresses with only 30 and 20 respectively. These kinds of findings might be useful to individuals in trying to identify the characteristics of a working environment which do or do not suit them. For example, we might be surprised if student no. 9, disliking working with technical equipment, was working in an intensive

Table 7.6 Master sheet of scores obtained by each item: group II

Item	Student no.									Total	Rank
	1	2	3	4	5	6	7	8	9		
Psychosocial factors											
1	250	250	250	250	250	250	250	250	250	2250	6
2	280	100	300	260	230	300	240	20	280	2010	9
3	50	100	290	200	260	310	500	350	380	2440	4
4	100	150	320	110	240	430	180	500	410	1090	14
5	410	50	180	300	250	100	230	270	230	2020	8
6	370	10	310	270	330	170	160	40	300	1960	10
7	220	20	270	360	200	120	270	350	370	2180	7
8	230	50	190	150	290	270	170	50	240	1640	12
Situational factors											
9	450	100	200	240	280	500	360	0	360	2490	3
10	400	100	240	280	270	200	370	90	390	1050	15
11	200	50	330	230	310	450	350	290	320	2530	2
12	300	70	360	350	340	350	310	80	400	2560	1
13	310	10	340	340	300	150	290	310	390	2430	5
14	150	10	90	100	220	130	400	480	220	1800	11
15	170	10	130	50	100	110	150	330	200	1250	13

Table 7.7 Mean scores indicating the more stressful factors for groups I and II

Group	Factors	
	Situational	Psychosocial
I	2490	2584
	(17430/7)	(20670/8)
II	2015	1924
	(14110/7)	(15390/8)

therapy unit. The individual profiles may in fact be more helpful to us from this practical than the finding that psychosocial factors are more stressful than situational ones, or vice versa.

There are a number of factors that we have not accounted for, but which may have affected our results. Our nurses represented all kinds of different types of nursing, from community to intensive therapy, and since they were all experienced it is likely that they were influenced by their varied work situations. If we had compared say surgical nurses with psychiatric nurses, we might have found that our results were much more clearly distinguishable. Similarly if we had involved students, who generally do not choose their wards, we might have found different results. You could test these ideas yourselves. The practical requires you to be rather creative in your thinking about stresses in nursing and you may feel that the lists our students compiled are not full enough or could be much more tightly defined. There are no right answers here. You must design lists that test what you want to investigate and involve as subjects the people you think will give you the most useful results. The main point is that you should feel able to investigate this very important area for yourself and in so doing perhaps learn more about yourself and your needs at work. Then, if you are discontented you can be active in trying to discover why and in identifying the characteristics of the sort of environment in which you would like to work. Obviously the characteristics of the environment are only part of the question, and in the next practical we will return to considering those factors specifically concerned with the individual.

Practical 7.3 Personal requirements for work satisfaction

Introduction

It is likely that our expectations of an occupation affect our experience of it. We discussed this in Chapter 2 in relation to the question of which people chose nursing as a career. In this chapter we are looking at stress and discontent among people who are nurses. An American study (Donovan 1980) investigated nurses' requirements for job satisfaction and tried to discover whether their career choice lived up to expectation. The nurses' highest priorities were for a sense of achievement, to be helpful, for stimulation, education and fellowship. However, they felt these expectations had not been met and were dissatisfied as a result. You could design a practical to investigate this yourself, based on Practical 3.1, in which you interviewed people about expectations and reality in becoming parents for the first time.

It may be quite difficult if you have been nursing for some time to think back to what your expectations were before you started nursing. You may be more interested in where your chosen career is going to lead you, whether or not you feel discontent with your work at the moment. You may well want to think about the future and the possibility of extending your experience. With this in mind, our final practical is a very personal one, aimed at helping you to assess yourself, your occupational needs and expectations, and in fact any other aspect of your life which you wish to include.

From childhood we become used to labelling 'what we want to be when we grow up' in very specific terms (e.g. engine driver, nurse, farmer) but it can be helpful to look at the question in a very different way. This involves thinking about and identifying the things in life which you feel are essential to you, which you could not do without, as well as other things you would like but do not consider essential. Having spent time working these things out about yourself you are then able to measure a variety of possibilities against your list. A simple non-career example would be to list all the things you must satisfy in the next house or flat you choose to live in (number of bedrooms, size of garden, distance from work), as well as all the less essential details. Then when you start to look you are quickly able to disregard those which do not fulfil your list of essential requirements, and you therefore save time and effort.

Method*

This is a practical that can be carried out by individuals working alone. It is very similar to many used by all sorts of people in planning their careers or making other decisions about their lives. It looks very simple, but may take time to complete, and is most helpful if you allow plenty of time and try to be very honest.

The idea is to make a list of say four items connected with working life, which you consider absolutely vital to your work satisfaction. These may refer to salary, whether you work alone or for someone else, when and where you want to work, whether you want holidays at specific times, how much pressure you are willing to accept, whether you want opportunities for further study, or travel and so on. You then make a second list consisting of all the other items, in some order of priority, which you would like to include but would not describe as essential. The list can be as flexible as you wish but should be as close a reflection of your own understanding of your occupational needs as you can manage.

---

*Practical based on an idea described by Derek Burden, Director of Imitax Ltd, consultants in organizational work design to the public service.

Results and discussion

To give you some idea of the range of topics you could take into account in this exercise, we will give you the anonymous lists of two individuals who managed to find occupations in nursing which they consider satisfy their requirements.

Subject no. I

Essential characteristics that the job *must* satisfy
Thinking job (involvement in planning, analysing, etc.)
Challenge
Possibility of further study within the job
My career development of concern to boss

Characteristics preferred but not necessarily essential
Building on existing nurse training
Nice place (not London)
Reasonable pay and prospects (i.e. could buy own house)
Be able to do relevant and useful research
Freedom at work to collaborate with others but also to get on alone

Subject no. II

Essential characteristics that the job *must* satisfy
Job that is more stimulating mentally, but not so demanding physically
Salary (specific amount)
Ability to institute change when required
Ongoing education including access to library and learning resources
Career prospects, scope to develop job
Regular hours, or preferably flexitime
Weekends off

Characteristics preferred but not necessarily essential
Be my own boss
Holidays when I want them
Location in price range for house buying, with easy access to countryside/sea
Town or city with good facilities for social life
Possibility for travel within UK and abroad

Now, instead of trying to think of a specific type of nursing you would like to do, you try to look at the characteristics of any type of nursing in a systematic way, looking beneath the surface of the label of the job, and trying to measure whether it meets your essential requirements. If it does, you compare it with your other requirements and this may help you to make an informed decision about yourself and your career. Some people find that simply thinking these things through to make the list is enough to help them know themselves better, and do not actually take their list with them to interviews. This is up to you.

If you find it very difficult to identify your needs in this way, you could use a checklist and sort it into your own order of priority. The list below is based on one as quoted by Burden (1975). It consists of items that are thought to be important psychological requirements of the content of a job. These are:

1. The need for the content of the work to be reasonably demanding (not just in terms of endurance)
2. To provide some variety
3. Opportunities to learn on the job and go on learning
4. Opportunities to make decisions and exercise discretion
5. Provision of social support and recognition
6. A sense of the job leading to some sort of desirable future

To use this, you could consider how important each is to you, and whether they are present in your work at the moment. If not, you could sort them into order of priority and look for them in any future area of work.

As in Practical 7.2 there can be no right or wrong answers. You must explore for yourself your needs, values and aspirations, and possibly also those of your family to try and make informed decisions. Hopefully the practical will help you to ensure that you choose the type of work which suits you, and if you have had doubts at times about nursing, for whatever reason, we hope these practicals will go some way toward helping you to identify the causes of your discontent and toward rectifying them.

Conclusion

In this chapter we have considered some factors which may be related to the quality of working life and job satisfaction for nurses. We have seen that the issue is not a straightforward one, with many factors to do with self and with work needing to be taken into account. We have assumed that stress and discontent among nurses is a special problem, but there is the possibility that stress among nurses is no different from that experienced by non-nurses. Carter (1982) draws attention to this possibility, suggesting that the problem of stress in nursing students has taken on mythical dimensions. Comparing American degree nurse-students with other undergraduates, she suggests that the stress may be a developmental crisis and not one actually dependent on being a nurse. We cannot ignore, however, the problems of wastage and absenteeism in nursing in the UK. Whatever the causes, we hope that individual nurses will find this chapter helpful in ensuring that the decisions which they make about their careers are good ones.

Summary

In this chapter we considered the problems of the work situation, specifically in relation to role conflict, psychosocial and situational factors linked with stress at work, and personal requirements for work satisfaction. In the first practical we used and developed Murray's (1983) rating scale to measure nurses' and the public's images of nurses. The second practical was based on Holmes & Rahe's (1967) method for compiling a life-events scale to enable us to identify the most stressful factors affecting nurses at work. The third practical required the reader to identify and list his or her own occupational requirements. This practical completes the practical section of the book by bringing the readers back to the need to understand themselves, both as nurses and as students of human behaviour. This was an important point made at the beginning of the book. However, in this chapter we have moved on from prescribing practicals designed by other people to help in self-awareness, to encouraging the reader to take a more creative role in the design of suitable practicals with a view to highlighting personal needs.

References

Berns, J S (1982) The application of job satisfaction theory to the nursing profession. *Nursing Leadership* 5, 27–33

Briggs, A (1972) *Report of the Committee on Nursing* London: HMSO

Burden, D W E (1975) The theoretical perspectives underlying the macrochange progress in Shell United Kingdom. In L E Davis & A B Cherns (eds) *The Quality of Working Life; Cases and Commentaries* vol. II. New York: Free Press

Carter, E W (1982) Stress in nursing students: dispelling some of the myth. *Nursing Outlook* 30, 248–252

Clark, J M & Redfern, S J (1978a) Absence and wastage in nursing – 1. *Nursing Times Occasional Papers* 74, 41–44

Clark, J M & Redfern, S J (1978b) Absence and wastage in nursing – 2. *Nursing Times Occasional Papers* 74, 45–48

Department of Health and Social Security (1982) *Nurse Manpower: Maintaining the Balance* London: HMSO

Donovan, L (1980) What nurses want (and what they're getting). *Registered Nurse* **4**, 22–30

Holmes, T H & Rahe, R H (1967) The Social Readjustment Rating Scale. *Journal of Psychosomatic Research* **11**, 213–218

Moores, B, Singh, B & Tun, A (1982) Attitudes of 2325 active and inactive nurses to aspects of their work. *Journal of Advanced Nursing* **8**, 29–31

Murray, M (1983) Role conflict and intention to leave nursing. *Journal of Advanced Nursing* **8**, 29–31

Nichols, K A, Springford, V & Searle, J (1981) An investigation of distress and discontent in various types of nursing. *Journal of Advanced Nursing* **6**, 311–318

Nursing Times (1983) Sharp rise in drop-out rate of learners. *Nursing Times* **79**, 20

Parkes, K R (1980a) Occupational stress among student nurses – 1. *Nursing Times Occasional Papers* **76**, 113–116

Parkes, K R (1980b) Occupational stress among student nurses – 2. *Nursing Times Occasional Papers* **76**, 117–119

Redfern, S J (1978) Absence and wastage in trained nurses: a selective review of the literature. *Journal of Advanced Nursing* **3**, 231–249

Smith, H L (1981) Nurses' quality of working life. *Nursing Research* **30**, 54–58

Tomlin, P J (1977) Psychological problems in intensive care. *British Medical Journal* **ii**, 441–443

Wallace, L M (1982) The heart of the matter: a clinical psychologist in coronary care. *Bulletin of the British Psychological Society* **35**, 379–383

CHAPTER 8

RESEARCHING INTO NURSING

The previous chapters have described several practicals set in the context of nursing to introduce the reader to relevant research findings of a psychological nature. In our final chapter we will consider these practicals in terms of the continuing development of 'research-mindedness' in nurses. We will consider some of the implications concerning nurses for undertaking research in real-life settings. Although there are no practicals, we will show you how to write up your own practicals and find your own way around research reports which have been published. For those who are keen to become more involved in research, we describe some initial steps for you to take.

Investigative techniques in psychology

In this book we have explored a wide variety of techniques which can be used to investigate human behaviour. Throughout we have tried to demonstrate how these techniques can be applied when researching into the field of nursing. The 17 practicals described in this book can, for convenience, be divided into five broad areas, although this categorization should not be seen to be exclusive. In undertaking any research there is clearly considerable overlap in the techniques adopted to address the question.

Two of our practicals were concerned with *observation*, a research tool which is perhaps not used as extensively as it might be. In Practical 1.1 you were asked to take part in a simple exercise involving searching for hazards in a line drawing of a ward situation. Here we were interested in the kind of factors which affected your performance. Practical 5.2 was far more structured and introduced you to the use of standardized and objective schedules for observing behaviour. The latter might be used to good effect in future research interested in how nurses actually carry out what they have been taught.

The book also introduced you to the use of *interviews* and *questionnaires*, including *rating scales*. Practical 3.1 gave you the opportunity to carry out an interview yourself. Here a set of questions had to be designed to enable you to draw out information from a subject in a face-to-face situation. The questionnaire you designed for Practical 3.2 was similar, although this technique requires even greater expertise with the design of questions. In this approach the only contact with your subject is through the questionnaire itself. Rating scales were discussed in Practicals 4.3 and 7.2. In Practical 4.3 you were introduced to a fairly conventional approach to scaling, which involved eliciting attitudes toward mentally retarded people. Attitudinal questions are often used in questionnaires and, more informally, in interviews. Practical 7.2 gave you practice in the design of a rating scale based on the original work of Holmes & Rahe (1967) first discussed in Chapter 3. This approach is rather more creative than the traditional design of attitude scales.

Practicals 4.1, 6.1, 6.2 and 7.1 demonstrated the use of the psychologist's most powerful technique, the *experiment*. In experiments one variable or factor is altered systematically to see the effect this has on another constant variable. The former is referred to in the literature as the independent variable, the latter as the dependent variable. For example, the dependent variable in Practical 4.1 was how nurses rated the patients. The independent variable was the diagnosis, which varied according to the information our subjects was given. We could have had a larger number of diagnoses (independent variables) to manipulate. Our results showed that the diagnosis (independent variable) affected how the patients were judged (the dependent variable). The main difficulty in using this technique is that it is not always possible to manipulate independent variables (e.g. different forms of treatment) in real life. Nevertheless, this approach is potentially the most useful tool available for finding out the causes of behaviour.

The difficulties in carrying out experimental work in everyday situations have led to the development of a variety of techniques which we can call *descriptive*. In Practical 2.1 you were invited to carry out a case study of yourself. The use of case studies is important, especially in those areas where the effects of intervention are being assessed (cf. Yule &

Hemsley 1977). Unfortunately, there is some confusion concerning whether case studies are objective or if in fact they are too subjective to be of value. As you will have seen from Practical 2.1, case studies can be carried out objectively. Furthermore, if designed appropriately, the experimental technique can be applied to the single case study. Practicals 3.3 and 4.2 introduced the use of content analysis, a descriptive but valuable technique. Similarly, the use of rank ordering was demonstrated in Practicals 4.2 and 5.1. This technique enables interesting comparisons to be made about the same data and readily lends itself to the experimental approach.

The fifth broad area can best be described as *experiential*. Throughout the book we have actively involved the reader in learning not only the content of psychology but its methods. All the practicals have given the reader the opportunity to function as a psychologist investigating nursing. Some practicals have been more experiential than others. Practical 5.3, for example, used role playing as a means of discovering more about human behaviour in the context of nursing. The final practical in the book stresses 'self-reflection' and, although similar to a case study, is intentionally more subjective and personal. We certainly do not advocate the use of experiential methods to the exclusion of the other techniques explained in this book, but we do feel that students studying psychology should be given some opportunity to find out more about themselves. This was the aim of our including some specific examples of the experiential approach. However, as for any practical in psychology, it is important to learn how to read published work in the area and how to write up your own reports. This is the aim of the section following.

Psychological research reports

You will have noticed that each time in this book we described and reported a particular practical, we followed a simple format, which included an introduction, method, results and discussion. When you read research papers in journals, you will find a similar pattern of reporting, although ours has been simplified. Knowing the typical format of research papers helps you to read them more efficiently and so we will include a brief description of each section. You will also find this useful if you decide to write up any of the practicals since it helps you to know in which order to describe what you did and what you found.

Title This is important and should state plainly the subject of study.

This is especially true when reports are published because, if someone needs to make use of the work for their own research or teaching purposes, they will need to know the key words associated with it. Cryptic or obscure titles can mean that the research is accidentally overlooked by other people.

Abstract Most published papers give an abstract after the title which briefly summarizes the content or findings. Although presented first in the article, it is often written up last so that it is a concise statement of the whole paper. In skimming through a number of articles you can read the abstracts to give you an immediate idea about whether a particular paper is going to be of use to you. If it is, you can read on, if not, no time has been wasted.

Introduction This usually follows the abstract and describes the previous work carried out in the field (similar to our chapter introductions). In major studies, such as those carried out in conjunction with the RCN, the introductions include an extensive review of the literature and this in itself can be a valuable source of information whether or not you yourself intend doing a research project on that topic. The introduction should also describe the reason for deciding to undertake the project and provide the rationale for the techniques selected.

Method This section includes details about the subjects involved in the study, any apparatus used (e.g. observation schedules, stopwatches) and a description of exactly how the research was done. One reason for this is so that others can replicate the study [as we did, e.g., in Practicals 7.1 and 7.2, using the work of Murray (1983) and that of Holmes & Rahe (1967)]. If a study can be replicated its reliability can be ascertained.

Results These are normally presented descriptively without any evaluative interpretations. Where possible, results should be tabulated or included in figures. Any statistical tests undertaken should be described here and the results presented. It should be possible to refer to this section and to find out quickly and easily the nature of the data collected.

Discussion However, it is in the discussion section that the researcher evaluates the results in the light of previous knowledge and the stated research problem. Any shortcomings are noted and the significance of the findings is considered. Suggestions may be made concerning ways of improving on the technique another time. Toward the end of this section, the findings are drawn together and the implications noted. This is often followed by a brief summary outlining the whole project.

Initially, many people simply read the title and abstract plus the summary, if there is one, to gain a rapid impression of a project as a way of determining its likely value to them. This can be also a way for nurses to keep up to date with the kinds of research which are being published without feeling they have to read every paper in detail. In the next section we will discuss the use of research literature as a further step in developing research-mindedness.

Where next?

Reading journals containing research data is very important in developing and maintaining research-mindedness. *Nursing Times* and *Nursing Mirror* frequently publish short articles from research studies and these are easily obtainable. In our book we have made frequent reference to other journals such as *Journal of Advanced Nursing* and *Nursing Research*. These, and several others, can be obtained from medical and nursing libraries. They can also be taken by individuals on a subscription basis and we list some addresses in Appendix VIII. One way of sustaining interest in journals is to start a 'journal club' among colleagues, perhaps study-block, ward or unit based, in which each person undertakes to read and report on all the papers published in one journal. You could meet every 1 or 2 months, depending on the frequency of publication. You don't just have to confine yourselves to nursing journals. We use medical and clinical speciality journals as well as scientific and behavioural science ones. This keeps us in touch with numerous developments reflecting the personal interests of participants.

If you have decided that you would like to know more about research, there are several courses of action open to you. One is to read some nursing research texts. Another is to begin to learn about more sophisticated techniques and statistics.

Statistical considerations   To concentrate on the research methods in this book, we have not emphasized the painstaking evaluation of findings which normally occurs in research. We have not investigated whether our results have been affected by chance. Normally we test findings using statistics to see if they are significant or have been affected by chance. If you would like to experiment with the statistical analysis of some practicals in this book, we list in Appendix VIII some statistical tests which could be applied to them. You will need a good statistics book, for example, Cohen & Holliday (1982), from which to follow the instructions rather like a recipe book.

Furthering your education It may be more appropriate, however, to consider taking a course to further your knowledge of research methods. These are available at several different levels. Many postregistration courses for nurses include research techniques and project work in their syllabuses, including, for example, the clinical nursing courses organized by the National Boards, the Diploma in Nursing and special degree courses in social research methods, for which grants can sometimes be obtained. The DHSS tries to support nurses in this respect and local authorities may also help. Many nurses undertake specific degrees associated with their nursing qualifications. Courses such as these are spread throughout the UK on both a full- or part-time basis and often include research methods. The Open University runs short research appreciation courses and nurses can also read for a degree in their spare time through the Open University. (For further information see Appendix VIII.)

By encouraging you to do practicals from this book, we have tried to give you the opportunity to discover for yourself ways in which behavioural research can be done. As you will have found, things do not always go according to plan and we recommend trial runs to iron out problems. These are known as pilot studies. The practicals, as such, have been no more than exercises in techniques, requiring practice to establish confidence and expertise. These have served the purpose of allowing you to gain expertise in situations in which it does not matter too much if things go wrong. In real research you cannot afford to take this sort of risk and this is one reason why safeguards such as those described in the next section exist.

Ethical considerations All researchers have important responsibilities toward their subjects and their discipline. Nurses also have special responsibilities toward their patients and their employers. Ethical principles were laid down for all researchers as a result of abuses to human subjects in the last World War. There is a detailed review of the subject by Gutteridge et al. (1982). Anyone who wishes to undertake research has a responsibility to familiarize themselves with ethical principles and RCN has published an important booklet on the subject entitled *Ethics Related*

to Research in Nursing (RCN 1977). This not only describes the responsibilities of nurse researchers, but also suggests that any nurse may at
times have to protect patients from inappropriate research. This would be
difficult if nurses had no appreciation of either the need for research or
the fact that sometimes it may conflict with the interests of the
patient.

The point is made in the booklet that 'the ethics of nursing research
must be consistent with the ethics of nursing practice' (p.1). To try and
ensure that, in practice, the two are consistent, hospitals usually set up
ethical committees to consider requests to carry out research. This
safeguard is important because patients, and sometimes staff, may feel
unable or unwilling to consent or in fact to decline from taking part in
the proposed research. It is important that these ethical committees
include an experienced behavioural scientist if they are to work effectively. The increasing interest in behavioural research as demonstrated in
this text, makes the inclusion of such a person crucial. Where the general
public are concerned, it is assumed that they are free to accept or decline
an invitation to participate in research. However, ethical principles must
still be observed. Informing the subject of the purpose and, at a later date,
findings of the study is one such principle which is easily overlooked, as it
is sometimes thought that the subjects will bias their responses as a result
of knowing the purpose of the project. It is customary for researchers to
have discussions with colleagues and seniors to ensure that the subjects,
future research in the area and the reputation of the discipline concerned
are not jeopardized through ignorance or thoughtlessness.

One can appreciate from this brief discussion that research should not
be undertaken lightly. However, if you feel you have a topic which you
would like to investigate, we would encourage you not to feel
overwhelmed by the prospect of doing so. There are people who are
qualified to advise you, such as Nursing Research Liaison Officers. The
roles for these officers are being developed and, by approaching the senior
nursing staff in your area, you will be able to find out who to contact.
You may also meet appropriate people through nursing research interest
groups and local branches of the RCN will be able to put you in touch
with such groups.

Conclusion

In this book we have concentrated on introducing you to the process of
research in the context of psychology and nursing. This is only a beginning, especially for those who are anxious to work beyond classroom

practicals toward real projects. In addition to showing you a range of techniques from psychology, we have described many research findings relevant to nurses. We hope this will have increased your interest in psychology and nursing and given you knowledge which you can begin to apply to your work. In particular, we hope it has served to increase your insight into human behaviour. There is a tradition in nursing of seeing things in very 'black and white' terms, but psychology demands that a range of possibilities be considered. Sometimes this can be difficult for nurses, making them unsure how to act. This is why the evaluation of one's work as a nurse and as a student of human behaviour is vitally important. If we do not evaluate the outcomes of the things we do or investigate, we can never measure which course of action is most appropriate under which conditions. Whenever possible, we should try to ensure that we act on the basis of knowledge, adopting a critical stance in the evaluation of our actions, to compare the outcomes with our goals. Clearly, the nursing process and the research process are similar in this respect and although, in this book, we have described research methods from a psychologist's perspective, they are in fact intrinsically related to the process of nursing.

Summary

The aims of this chapter were to summarize the investigative techniques described throughout the book, to give some guidelines for reading and writing research reports and to suggest ways in which nurses can take steps to further their understanding of research. The chapter included references to numerous resources which are listed in Appendix VIII and which it is hoped may assist nurses in the attainment of research-mindedness.

References

Cohen, L & Holliday, M (1982) *Statistics for Social Scientists. An Introductory Text with Computer Programs in BASIC* London: Harper and Row

Gutteridge, F, Bankowski, Z, Curran, W & Dunne, J (1982) The structure and functioning of ethical review committees. *Social Science and Medicine* **16**, 1791–1800

Holmes, T H & Rahe, R H (1967) The Social Readjustment Rating Scale. *Journal of Psychosomatic Research* **11**, 213–218

Murray, M (1983) Role conflict and intention to leave nursing. *Journal of Advanced Nursing* **8**, 29–31

Royal College of Nursing (1977) *Ethics Related to Research in Nursing* London: Royal College of Nursing

Yule, W & Helmsley, D (1977) Single case method in medical psychology. In S Rachman (ed.) *Contributions to Medical Psychology* vol. 1. Oxford: Pergamon

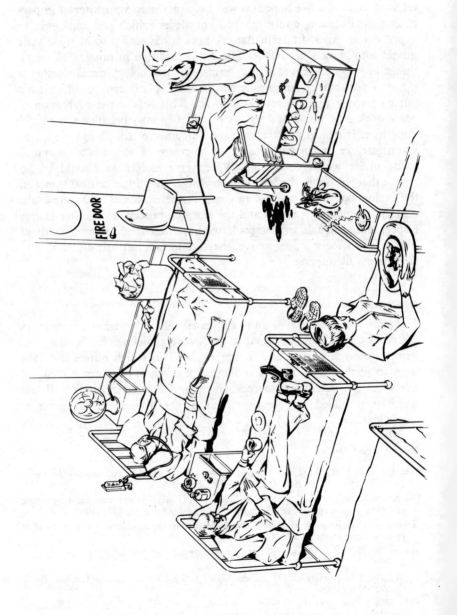

Appendix II   Scoring keys for Practical 2.1

Below are shown the scoring keys for the personality tests used in Practical 2.1 with some guidelines for interpreting the results.

GENERALIZED EXPECTANCY FOR SUCCESS SCALE — SCORING KEY

To compute your total score on the expectancy for success scale, first REVERSE the scores for the following thirteen items (change a 1 to a 5, a 2 to a 4, leave a 3 alone, change a 4 to a 2, and a 5 to a 1):

   items 1, 2, 4, 6, 7, 8, 14,
   15, 17, 18, 24, 27 and 28

Note that the possible range of test scores varies from 30 to 150. The higher your score, the greater your expectancy for success in the future.

Fibel & Hale (1978) administered this test to American undergraduate students in psychology courses and found that the women's scores ranged from 65 to 143, and the men's scores ranged from 81 to 138. The average score for both men and women was 112 (112.32 for women and 112.15 for men).

EXTROVERSION–INTROVERSION — SCORING KEY

To find your total score simply award yourself one point if your answer corresponds to the key shown below. For example, if you put 'YES' to question 1 score one point. The higher you score the more extrovert you are.

1. YES	2. YES	3. NO	4. YES	5. YES	6. YES
7. NO	8. YES	9. NO	10. YES	11. YES	12. YES
13. NO	14. NO	15. NO	16. NO	17. YES	18. NO
19. YES	20. YES	21. YES	22. NO	23. YES	24. YES

In the manual for the test Eysenck & Eysenck (1964) report that the average score for a group of student nurses with an average age of 20 years, was 12.4. Qualified nurses aged approximately 26 years, scored on average 12.6. The most extroverted groups were engineering apprentices, salesmen and student occupational therapists. The most introverted groups were clerks, teachers and students.

INTERNAL–EXTERNAL CONTROL — SCORING KEY

The statements in the left-hand column reflect internal control, those in the right-hand column external control. By subtracting the number of statements marked in the left-hand column for the number marked in the right-hand column, you can get a score of the extent to which you believe that rewards come from your own behaviour or from external sources. A full scoring key is shown below.

10	I	0	E	= 10	I
9	I	1	E	= 8	I
8	I	2	E	= 6	I
7	I	3	E	= 4	I
6	I	4	E	= 2	I
5	I	5	E	= 0	
4	I	6	E	= 2	E
3	I	7	E	= 4	E
2	I	8	E	= 6	E
1	I	9	E	= 8	E
0	I	10	E	= 10	E

ASSERTIVENESS INVENTORY — SCORING KEY

To find your total concerning the degree of discomfort felt in this wide range of situations simply add all your scores together. The higher your score the more discomfort you would feel. Use the same procedure to find the overall likelihood of behaving in these ways. The higher your score the less likely you are to display this kind of behaviours.

In their standardization of this test Gambrill & Richey (1975) found that the average score for both men and women was about 96 on the scale measuring discomfort and about 106 on the scale measuring response probability. It was generally found that total discomfort scores were lower than response probability scores. Their sample consisted of American undergraduates studying social science.

Appendix III   Patient portrait for Practical 4.1

Is 54 years old
Married with three children
Served in forces
Votes labour
Owns semi-detached house
Keen on sport
Occupation: technician

Reason for hospitalization:
hernia repair

Appendix III   Patient portraits for Practical 4.1

Is 54 years old
Married with three children
Served in forces
Votes labour
Owns semi-detached house
Keen on sport
Occupation: technician

Reasons for hospitalization:
cirrhosis of the liver

Appendix IV   Scripts for Practical 5.3

Scripts for role play A. Player 1
You are: Sister/charge nurse in a very busy surgical ward. Today 10 patients will have operations under general anaesthetic. Most patients stay in for 4–7 days. The turnover is very high and you seem to be chronically short-staffed. Mrs Scale is a rather obese middle-aged lady who never seems to be satisfied with what the nurses try to do for her. She had a hernia repair 2 weeks ago, complains continually of pain, is very difficult to mobilize and is now showing signs of a chest infection. She tends to spend all day in bed, looking as though she is asleep and is often rude when nurses approach her. Her husband visits irregularly and seems to smell of drink. It has been decided that the patient should be escorted on walks around the hospital to try and speed up mobilization and try to raise her morale by a change of scenery. You decide to start this now.

Scripts for role play A. Player 2

You are: Mrs Scale. You've had a large and troublesome hernia for years
and eventually went to the doctor about it. He arranged for its cor-
rection by a major operation (it must have been bad because
you've been in hospital over 2 weeks and there's no hope of your
going home yet). The stitches don't look healed properly so when
you stand up you think all your insides will fall out and make a lot
of mess and work for the nurses and doctors. And there's this
chronic pain in your hip. It's got much worse since you came into
hospital, in fact you can hardly bear to put your foot down. It
nearly makes you cry. Sid (your husband), is not coping too well at
home with the youngest (been in trouble with the police already)
and Sid says it's driving him to drink. Oh well, as long as you can
just lie here and get your strength back, you'll be alright.

Scripts for role play B. Players 1 and 2

You are: Staff nurses newly appointed to the geriatric unit. Mr Brown is to have two suppositories as he seems to be constipated. He is apparently rather deaf. He usually lives with his daughter, who is having a 2-week holiday and he does not appear to know where he is.

Scripts for role play B. Player 3

You are: Denis Brown, aged 88 years and extremely deaf. There's something not quite right about where you are . . . perhaps your daughter's redecorated the sitting room (must remember to ask her). Your familiar routine isn't quite right, though quite what is wrong you haven't yet worked out. Everyone seems to be wearing silly hats – perhaps it's a party – yes that would be it. Edith (your daughter) said something about a party. Well, if it's a party you wish you could eat better, but there's these awful crampings in your stomach and your mouth's so dry.

Scripts for role play C. Player 1

You are: Sister/charge nurse in a very busy surgical ward. Mrs Lowther is a young mother of three who has had a cholecystectomy. She returned from theatre 6 hours ago. You arrive on duty and, while checking all the patients, notice that she is restless and sweaty. In your opinion, her prescription for analgesia is inadequate and a stronger drug should be used. You find the Houseman, Dylan Branwell, a newly qualified doctor (who is desperately busy trying to perform venepuncture on a deteriorating patient) and start to ask him about Mrs Lowther's analgesia.

Scripts for role play C. Player 2

You are: Dylan Branwell, a newly qualified doctor. This is your first surgical house job and the Consultant works at all hours of the day and night and expects you to keep up. There were several minor operations and a cholecystectomy this morning (gosh, you must remember to check her) and now yesterday's emergency gastrectomy is deteriorating and you can't find a decent vein to restart the intravenous infusion. You haven't slept for about 36 hours and sister/charge nurse seems to know more than you do. (In fact it might be sensible to leave her in charge anyway; as it is, you have to ask about almost everything.)

Appendix V   List A for Practical 6.1
1. Vein
2. Duodenum
3. Colon
4. Ovary
5. Plasma
6. Lymphocyte
7. Retina
8. Ureter
9. Pleura
10. Dermis
11. Larynx
12. Sacrum
13. Patella
14. Dendrite
15. Atrium

Appendix VI   Response slips, list B and instructions for Practical 6.2

Response slips for group 'CS' and group 'ES'

'CS'	Trial no.	'ES'	Trial no.
1		1	
2		2	
3		3	
4		4	
5		5	
6		6	
7		7	
8		8	
9		9	
10		10	
11		11	
12		12	
13		13	
14		14	
15		15	
16		16	
17		17	
18		18	
19		19	
20		20	
21		21	
22		22	
23		23	
24		24	

List B

Epilepsy
Diabetes
Colitis
Virus
Ulcer
Insomnia
Yellow fever
Rheumatism
Warts
Gangrene
Pneumonia
Measles
Laryngitis
Jaundice
Fainting
Tonsilitis
Amnesia
Nausea
Sinusitis
Bronchitis
Ketonuria
Quinsy
Oedema
Hay fever

Instructions for group 'ES' and group 'CS'

'ES'

Try to organize your recalled words alphabetically. When you look at the words, note their first letters and make an attempt to associate the word with the letter. When you write down the words, go through the letters of the alphabet one at a time and try to remember the word that goes with each letter.

'CS'

This is to inform you that you have been assigned to experimental group 'CS'. You should continue as before, trying to do your very best on each recall trial and put down as many words from the list as you possibly can.

Appendix VII   List C for Practical 6.3

Anthisan
Chloromycetin
Diconal
Depixol
Dromoran
Omnopon
Aludrox SA
Dulcolax
Flagyl
Physeptone
Mandrax
Cedilanid
Dexedrine
Inderal
Mogadon
Phenergan
Butazolidin
Dipidolor
Lasix
Narphen
Amoxil
Pethilorfan
Ventolin
Valium
Welldorm

Appendix VIII Further resources
Addresses

The addresses below are those of the publishers of each journal.

Nursing

Journal of Advanced Nursing
Blackwell Scientific Publications Ltd
PO Box 88
Oxford

Nursing Research
555 West 57th Street
New York
NY 10019

Nursing
Pembroke House
36/37 Pembroke Street
Oxford OX1 1BL

International Journal of Nursing Studies
Pergamon Press Ltd
Headington Hill Hall
Oxford OX3 OBW

Nursing Times
Macmillan Journals Ltd
4 Little Essex Street
London WC2R 3LF

Nursing Mirror
Surrey House
1 Throwley Way
Sutton
Surrey SM1 4QQ

American Journal of Nursing
555 West 57th Street
New York
NY 10019

Nurse Education Today
Longman Group Ltd
Fourth Avenue
Harlow
Essex CM19 5AA

Psychology

The journals listed below often contain one or more articles of interest to nurses. This is a selected list and there are many other journals which may sometimes be helpful. These journals may be found in university, hospital or college libraries.

British Journal of Psychology
British Journal of Clinical Psychology
British Journal of Developmental Psychology
British Journal of Medical Psychology
British Journal of Social Psychology

British Psychological Society
St Andrew's House
48 Princess Road East
Leicester LE1 7DR

Social Science and Medicine
Journal of Psychosomatic Research
Pergamon Press Ltd
Headington Hill Hall
Oxford OX3 OBW

Statistics

The following statistical tests can be carried out on the practicals listed below. Page numbers refer to Cohen & Holliday (1982), who provide a 'step-by-step' guide to help you.

Practicals 6.2, 6.3 and 7.1: Student's *t* test for independent samples, pp.230–234. (Own self-image vs public-image; perceived public-image vs public-image.)
Practical 1.1: Mann–Whitney *U* test, pp.235–241.
Practical 7.1: Student's *t* test for correlated means (matched groups), pp.190–192. (Own self-image vs perceived public-image.)
Practical 7.1: Wilcoxon's matched-pairs signed-ranks test (matched groups), pp.193–197.
Practicals 2.1 and 5.1: Spearman rank-order correlation coefficient, pp.152–156.
Practical 4.3: Chi-squared, pp.243–244 (with reference to the data in Table 4.3).

Cohen, L & Holliday, M (1982) *Statistics for Social Scientists* An Introductory Text with Computer Programs in BASIC London: Harper and Row.

Educational resources

Chief Nursing Officer (Education)
Department of Health and Social Security
Hannibal House
Elephant and Castle
London SE1 6BY

Addresses for specific courses in colleges and universities can be obtained from local public libraries.

Open University
Walton Hall
Milton Keynes MK7 6AF

Details of courses for nurses run in your area (e.g. Diploma in Nursing) and of nursing personnel (e.g. Research Liaison Officers) should be obtainable from the appropriate Schools of Nursing or senior nursing staff.

INDEX

Behavioural Treatment of Problem Children

A PRACTICE MANUAL